# Is Nothing Sacred?

'I do feel a sense of the sacred in a number of respects and I could quote other scientists who feel the same.' *Richard Dawkins*

We call many things sacred, from churches to cows and flags to burial grounds. But is it still meaningful to talk of things being sacred, or is the idea a relic of a bygone religious age? Does everything – and every life – have its price, or are some things sacrosanct? *Is Nothing Sacred?* is a stimulating and wide-ranging exploration of why and how we should value human life, art, the environment and personal freedom.

In a series of lucid but controversial essays, leading philosophers debate whether there is a right to die, whether we should preserve the giant California redwoods, cherish Vermeer's originals for their own sake or curtail personal freedom for the greater good. Ronald Dworkin argues that the concept of the sacred is essential to any human ethics, and Simon Blackburn explains why he thinks 'a humanist should not feel guilty at the emotions of awe and reverence that can be inspired by great religious works of art'.

*Is Nothing Sacred?* brings together outstanding philosophers and thinkers to discuss this much-talked about but little understood question, including: Suzanne Uniacke, Michael Clark, Alan Holland, Simon Blackburn, Richard Dawkins, Richard Norman, Alan Haworth, Nigel Warburton, Matthew Kieran, John Harris and Ronald Dworkin.

**Ben Rogers** is the author of *Pascal: In Praise of Vanity, A.J. Ayer: A Life*, and *Beef and Liberty*. He is Senior ~~~ ellow at the Institute for Public Pol~~ ~~ or a wide range of newspapers a

# Is **Nothing** Sacred?

Edited by Ben Rogers

Routledge
Taylor & Francis Group

LONDON AND NEW YORK

First published 2004
by Routledge
2 Park Square, Milton Park, Abingdon, Oxfordshire, OX14 4RN

Simultaneously published in the USA and Canada
by Routledge
29 West 35th Street, New York, NY 10001

*Routledge is an imprint of the Taylor & Francis Group*

Typeset in DIN and Minion by RefineCatch Limited, Bungay, Suffolk
Printed and bound in Great Britain by TJ International Ltd, Padstow, Cornwall

*British Library Cataloguing in Publication Data*
A catalogue record for this book is available from the British Library

*Library of Congress Cataloging in Publication Data*
A catalog record for this book has been requested

100 55 P-1 997

ISBN 0-415-30483-0 (hbk)
ISBN 0-415-30484-9 (pbk)

# Contents

# Contributors

**Piers Benn** is Lecturer in Medical Ethics at Imperial College London. He is author of *Ethics* (UCL Press 1998 and Routledge 2003). He is particularly interested in ethics and philosophy of religion.

**Simon Blackburn** is Professor of Philosophy at the University of Cambridge. His books include *Essays in Quasi-realism* (1993), *Ruling Passions* (1998) and two bestselling introductions to philosophy, *Think* (1999) and *Being Good* (2001).

**Michael Clark** is Professor of Philosophy at the University of Nottingham and editor of *Analysis*. He recently published *Paradoxes from A to Z* (Routledge).

**Richard Dawkins** was educated at Oxford University and has taught zoology at the universities of California and Oxford. He is the Charles Simonyi Professor of the Public Understanding of Science at Oxford University. His books about evolution and science include *The Selfish Gene, The Blind Watchmaker, River out of Eden, Climbing Mount Improbable* and, most recently, *Unweaving the Rainbow*.

**Ronald Dworkin** is Sommer Professor of Law and Philosophy at New York University and Quain Professor of Jurisprudence at University College London. He is author of many influential books on political philosophy, jurisprudence and ethics, including *Taking Rights Seriously, Life's Dominion, Law's Empire* and *Sovereign Virtue: The Theory and Practice of Equality.*

**Simona Giordano** is Marie Curie Postdoctoral Research Fellow at The Institute of Medicine, Law and Bioethics at the University of Manchester. She has published widely on psychiatric ethics and on medical humanities and issues concerning ageing.

**John Harris** is Sir David Alliance Professor of Bioethics, University of Manchester, and a member of the United Kingdom Genetics Commission since its foundation in 1999. Recent publications include *Clones, Genes and Immortality* (Oxford University Press, 1998), *Bioethics* (Oxford University Press, 2001) and (with Justine C. Burley) *A Companion To Genethics: Philosophy and the Genetic Revolution* (Blackwell, 2002).

**Alan Haworth** teaches Political Philosophy and the History of Ideas at London Metropolitan University. His books include *Free Speech* (Routledge, 1998) and *Understanding the Political Philosophers: From Ancient to Modern Times* (Routledge, 2003).

**Alan Holland** is Professor Emeritus at Lancaster University and editor of the interdisciplinary journal *Environmental Values.* His recent publications cover a range of topics in 'applied' philosophy, including sustainability, decision-making and genetic handicap. He currently serves on the Home Office Animal Procedures Committee.

**Matthew Kieran** is Lecturer in Philosophy at the University of Leeds. He publishes in aesthetics and ethics and is the author of *Revealing Art* (Routledge, 2004).

**Richard Norman** was formerly Professor of Moral Philosophy at the University of Kent and now teaches part-time at the university. His philosophical publications include the books *The Moral Philosophers* and *Free and Equal* (both published by Oxford University Press), and *Ethics, Killing and War* (published by Cambridge University Press). His forthcoming book *On Humanism* will be published by Routledge. He is a member of the British Humanist Association and of East Kent Humanists.

**Ben Rogers** is a Senior Research Fellow at the Institute for Public Policy Research, London. He is author of *Pascal: In Praise of Vanity* (Orion), *A.J. Ayer: A Life* (Vintage and Grove Atlantic) and *Beef and Liberty* (Chatto).

**Suzanne Uniacke** is Reader in Applied Ethics at the University of Hull. Before moving to the United Kingdom in 2001 she taught philosophy in Australia. She has published widely in ethics, applied ethics and philosophy of law.

**Nigel Warburton** is Senior Lecturer in Philosophy at the Open University and a member of the Humanist Philosophers' Group. His most recent books are *The Art Question* (Routledge, 2003) and *Ernö Goldfinger: The Life of an Architect* (Routledge, 2004).

# Preface and Acknowledgements

The essays in this collection originated in a conference held at King's College London in October 2001 on the theme 'Is Nothing Sacred?' The conference was organised by the British Humanist Association on behalf of the Humanist Philosophers' Group. This group of mainly professional philosophers has been meeting and exchanging e-mails on an e-group, under the aegis of the British Humanist Association, for over three years. It has produced, along the way, a number of short pamphlets, articles, and magazine features on topics of concern to atheists and humanists: paternalism, religious schools, creationism, and death and dying, to name a few.

Many of us who attended the conference found it more than usually stimulating, and we were delighted when Tony Bruce, head of philosophy at Routledge, offered to publish a book based on it. I, the British Humanist Association and the Humanist Philosophers' Group would like to express our thanks to all those who contributed to the conference and to this book. We are particularly grateful to Susan Uniacke, Simona Giordano, John Harris and Ronald Dworkin, who didn't attend the conference, but nevertheless agreed to contribute essays and comments to our publication.

We would also like to thank Robert Ashby, Hanne Stintson, Marilyn Mason and Madeleine Pym from the British Humanist

Association for all the support they have given the Humanist Philosophers' Group.

Finally, and on a personal note, I would like to thank Harriet Gugenheim for her forbearance.

Ben Rogers
November 2003

# Introduction

## Ben Rogers

All of these essays might be seen as wrestling with a single and very knotty problem – not so much a problem, in fact, more a predicament. All the writers are agnostics, most are atheists. They are not persuaded by any of the arguments for the existence of God, or the truth of any religions. They do not, for the most part, find they need to make use of religious concepts. They can get on just fine without believing in the divine godhead, the devil, or the existence of supernatural or transcendent realms. Yet most of them do not find it easy simply to jettison the concept of the sacred. As Richard Dawkins, perhaps the most renowned freethinker of our times, admits, there are some things he can't but feel are sacred: the Grand Canyon, early human skulls and important fossils. At the very least, many of these writers worry that viewing everything on a level – as uniformly profane, perhaps, or at least secular – would represent a real impoverishment in moral outlook.

As readers will discover, the contributors gathered here respond in very different ways to the mixed feelings that the concept of the sacred arouses in them. At the outset, however, it might be worth asking why this concept should pose the difficulty that it does to non-believers. Why should it continue, despite its obvious religious connotations, to retain at least some degree of purchase on them?

The answer, I believe, goes to the very heart of our nature as ethical, valuing beings. A hugely influential seam of modern ethics suggests that value is a single, homogeneous thing – that there exists a common scale or currency on which the value of everything can be measured. Moreover, though philosophers who adhere to this outlook disagree on the precise nature of the currency – some, for instance, identify it with happiness or utility, others with the satisfaction of preferences – they all tend to locate it in one subjective mental state or another. This is clearly true of utilitarianism, currently making something of a philosophical comeback, but it is no less true of a great deal of mainstream economic thinking (for utilitarianism see Layard 2003). The widespread commitment to free markets is based, at least in part, on the belief that to the extent that they optimise preference satisfaction, they optimise value itself. Cost–benefit analysis – still a flourishing economic discipline – is similarly premised on the belief that the value of everything – even public goods that cannot be effectively provided by the free market – can be cashed out on a single scale. So the benefits and costs of building, say, a dam that would provide plentiful cheap electricity, but destroy an eco-system, are reduced to a hypothesised 'willingness to pay' on the part of all those affected.

There is no denying the appeal of this way of thinking. It offers us the promise of a neat and tidy moral calculus. At the same time, it seems to get important things wrong. There are many things, after all, that we don't value according to their capacity to satisfy preferences or promote our happiness. We value them for themselves and want to say that they have an 'intrinsic' value. In fact we tend to evaluate the worth of preferences and ultimately of individual humans by reference to these highly valued things. I think less of someone, and would think less of myself, were I persuaded that his, her, my preferences and ethical judgements failed to honour those things I think intrinsically important.

I am not claiming that we value everything in this way. On the contrary, there are many things that we do value by reference to personal desires or more or less appetitive preferences. This is true of most of the common commodities, for instance, for sale on the market. It would be odd to say that apples and oranges have an intrinsic value. We don't think less of people who prefer one to the other, or like neither. But there is an important range of goods that we value not by reference to happiness or preference satisfaction, but in themselves. Typically, moreover, we define their value precisely in opposition to these lower goods whose value is a function of our appetites and desires. So what distinguishes goods with especially high or intrinsic value from ordinary, everyday goods, is that while we find it natural and acceptable to make trade-offs among the latter, we don't among the former. We would judge someone who treated everything as apples and oranges, that is, as essentially substitutable one for another, or of a like kind with everything else, as being ethically blind. We are happy to allow a trade in clothes, but not the people they cloth, in postcards but not the historic buildings or sublime landscapes they depict, in religious trinkets but not great religious works of art.

There are many ways that we can capture the distinction of worth that I am alluding to here. We can describe things, as I have already done, as having 'intrinsic' or 'instrumental' value, or as being 'high' or 'low', as being 'inviolable' or everyday. We can talk with the philosopher Charles Taylor about 'strongly' and 'weakly' valued goods (Taylor 1985a, especially essays 1 and 2). Or we can use the language of the market, describing strongly valued things as 'invaluable' or 'priceless', so drawing an implicit contrast with things that have a price. But I want to suggest that the main reason that many even avowedly anti-religious philosophers can't quite stop talking about things being 'sacred' or 'sacrosanct' (and relatedly, 'mundane' or 'profane') is that these quasi-religious concepts offer them another powerful way to articulate this fundamental distinction between different forms of worth. This quasi-religious language helps us articulate those contrasts 'between things which are recognised as of categoric or unconditioned or higher importance ... and things ... of lesser value'. And these distinctions in turn are, as Taylor has argued, a necessary feature of any ethics we would recognise as human (Taylor 1985b: 3).

It is sometimes suggested that all this talk of sacred objects and sacrosanct principles is so much empty rhetoric. We affirm that things are priceless, sacrosanct, inviolable, but then often give them up none-theless. Indeed, we often find ourselves in a position where we have to destroy or forgo some great good to save another – it might be said, to put it grandly, that this is an essential aspect of humanity's tragic pre-dicament. We give up some degree of freedom for security, or make choices between demands of family or friendship and the larger common good, to take just two examples.

But it is wrong to think that this proves that talk of sacredness is so much highfalutin hokum or poses a challenge to the distinction between strongly and weakly valued goods. For the choices we make between sacred or 'priceless' things are of a very different nature from the ones we make between lower, weakly valued goods. These latter tend to be easy precisely because we can measure them on a single, more or less utilitarian scale. We can rank them according to their ability to make us happy or satisfy preferences. But we have no ready way of ranking strongly valued goods; they are, in the philosophical jargon, 'incommensurate'. It is this that explains why choices between these sorts of goods are often so hard and why the choice, when made, often feels more or less arbitrary. And this too explains why, even as we give up one highly valued thing for another, we remain indebted or committed to the thing given up – a phenomenon that has no counterpart in the choices we make between weakly valued goods. We talk naturally about 'trading off' weakly valued things against each other, but applying this language to goods with an unconditional value feels inappropriate – almost sacrilegious. Instead the decision between strongly valued goods tends to have the character of a 'sacrifice' (another term with religious connotations).

Thus when we describe things as sacred, sacrosanct, inviolable, we mean, in fact, that they are 'inviolable except as a last resort'. That is why, as Suzanne Uniacke contends, the question whether life is sacred, is distinct from the question whether it is ever permissible to kill. In describing life as sacred we are not necessarily denying that it is sometimes permissible, or even right, to kill – in self-defence, to defend innocent people, or perhaps to relieve someone's suffering. We are, more normally, saying, instead, that killing should only be done as a last resort, and with a recognition, expressed among other things in enduring remorse, that something grave and regrettable, even wrongful, has been done.

I have suggested that most of the contributors to this volume, even though they are atheists, are not altogether happy to jettison the concept of the sacred and indicated why this might be so. It would be misleading to suggest, however, that they all think about the sacred in the same way. None seem tempted by the view that all values can be measured on a single profane scale – certainly none affirm such a view here. And most take the view that the concept can be freed from its religious roots and given a place in a secular ethics. They point out that most dictionary definitions allow 'sacred' to have non-religious as well as religious meanings. Even among these, however, there are differences of approach. Richard Norman, while allowing that human life is sacred, denies that nature can be. And Alan Howarth doesn't commit himself one way or the other, offering instead a considered examination of the question whether all reasonable people are bound to attach a supreme value to liberty.

But a minority of contributors – most notably Nigel Warburton and Michael Clark – argue that the concept of the sacred is irredeemably religious, and that non-believers should make do without it. They would prefer to see language purged of all religious vestiges, even if, as a result, it loses some of its evaluative force.

The tensions I have tried to gesture to here – between an atheistic suspicion of religious or quasi-religious concepts and a belief, constitutive of human nature itself, in the objective value of certain 'sacred' things – pull these writers in very different directions. Readers will want to find out whom they are most inclined to follow.

## References

Layard, Richard (2003) *Happiness: Has Social Science a Clue?* Lionel Robins Lectures, cep.lse.ac.uk/events/lectures/layard/RL030303.pdf

Taylor, Charles (1985a) *Human Agency and Language, Philosophical Papers 1*, Cambridge.

Taylor, Charles (1985b) *Philosophy and the Human Sciences, Philosophical Papers 2*, Cambridge.

# 1  Nature, Science, and the Sacred

## Richard Norman

Do we still need the idea of 'the sacred'? It is often suggested that one area in which we need to retain such language is that of our relationship to the natural world. We should not, it is said, regard nature merely as something to be manipulated for our own human purposes, but as something to be respected in its own right, and talk of nature as 'sacred' is thought to be an appropriate way of expressing this idea. In this chapter I shall give due weight to such concerns, but I shall argue that there are other and better ways of capturing the kind of value which we can and should attribute to the natural world.

## Is Nature Sacred?

If we are to reverse the destruction of the natural environment, do we need a new attitude to nature – or at any rate the revival of an old and discarded one? Some think that we do. In a Reith Lecture given on the radio in May 2000, the Prince of Wales suggested that

> if we are to achieve genuinely sustainable development we will first have to rediscover, or re-acknowledge, a sense of the sacred in our dealings with the natural world, and with each other. If literally nothing is held sacred any more –

because it is considered synonymous with superstition or in some other way 'irrational' – what is there to prevent us treating our entire world as some 'great laboratory of life', with potentially disastrous long-term consequences? Fundamentally, an understanding of the sacred helps us to acknowledge that there are bounds of balance, order and harmony in the natural world which set limits to our ambitions, and define the parameters of sustainable development.[1]

The contrast here is between what we might call an 'instrumental' attitude to nature, treating it as something we can use and control to our advantage, and a sense of nature as 'sacred'. There is however an obvious problem with Prince Charles's advocacy of 'a sense of the sacred'. The reasons which he gives are themselves, in part, instrumental ones. He warns that our current attitudes may have 'potentially disastrous long-term consequences' for the environment and for human beings who depend on it, and he argues for 'a cautious approach' which will help to ensure 'the preservation of bio-diversity and traditional communities'.[2] If that, however, is the nature of his, and our, concern, then it looks as though what we need is simply the application of what has been called the 'precautionary principle'. The Prince's 'sense of the sacred', if defended in instrumental terms, apparently turns out to be just a strong version of the precautionary principle: don't mess about with nature, exercise extreme caution in attempts to manipulate nature for human purposes, and cultivate strong inhibitions against doing so.

To call this 'a sense of the sacred' would surely be a misnomer. If we are looking for reasons for rediscovering a sense of the sacred in our dealings with the natural world, then the only good reason would be that nature *really is sacred.* And if the appeal to 'disastrous long-term consequences' is relevant at all, that can only be because a sense of the sacred in some way underlies and explains our understanding of what would be disastrous about certain kinds of consequences.

Is that in fact so? Think of the kinds of disastrous long-term consequences which are typically invoked to express concern about the destruction of the natural environment – the pollution of rivers, the disappearance of woodlands, soil erosion, long-term climate change leading to widespread flooding. What is it that we see as disastrous about this? Is it that rivers and woods, the soil and the climate are sacred, and that in bringing about these consequences we would have violated their sacred character? Do we need a 'sense of the sacred' to explain what would be bad about these outcomes?

At this point we need a clearer definition of what is distinctive about talk of 'the sacred', and a useful source here is the discussion of the idea that 'life is sacred' in Ronald Dworkin's influential book *Life's Dominion.*[3] Dworkin follows the standard distinction between 'intrinsic value' (what we value for its own sake) and 'instrumental value' (what we value as a means to something else), and he then distinguishes between two kinds of intrinsic value which he refers to as 'incremental value' and as 'the sacred'. Something has incremental value if, in valuing it, we want more of it, no matter how much we already have. Dworkin's example is the value of *knowledge.* To value knowledge is to want to promote it, to increase the amount of it. To talk of the intrinsic value of human life, in contrast, is to talk of a different kind of value. It is not that we want there to be as much of it existing as possible. We value it when and because it already exists, and that is the kind of value which we characteristically express by talking of something as 'sacred'. As well as the example of human life, Dworkin also cites the examples of works of art, and natural species, as things which we value as sacred rather than as having incremental value, and both examples will be pertinent to my own further argument. To regard something as sacred, he says, is to regard it as *inviolable*, as something which may not be destroyed once it exists.

It is this idea of 'inviolability' that seems to me to be the key. What is distinctive about 'the sacred' is that it sets up boundaries or barriers which must not be crossed. This fits well with Prince Charles's suggestion that 'an understanding of the sacred helps us to acknowledge that there are bounds of balance, order and harmony in the natural world which set limits to our ambitions'. To regard nature as sacred is to think of it as something on which we should not intrude. We should not apply our knowledge of nature and its causal laws simply in order to use it for human purposes.

This gives us a relatively clear idea of what we are talking about, but if that is what we mean by 'the sacred', then I want to go on to say that I do not think it is possible for us to recover that kind of relationship to the natural world. We know too much. Our power over nature is by now too great for it to be possible for us to relinquish it. Consider again some of the standard examples of concerns about the degradation of nature. If we are worried about carbon dioxide emissions, or the pollution of rivers, or the damage to the ozone layer, we cannot just step back from the problems and say that from now on we are going to treat these features of nature as sacred and not intrude on them. Our attitude is bound to be: How can we prevent pollution? How can we restore the quality of the water in our rivers? How can we reduce carbon emissions? How can we repair the hole in the ozone layer, or at least prevent it getting bigger? These questions all presuppose the standpoint of instrumental rationality. In posing them and trying to answer them, we draw on our scientific understanding, our knowledge of causal relationships, in order to decide how to act on nature most effectively to produce the most desirable results. And to think of nature in these terms is *not* to think of it as something sacred and inviolable.

I said that the recovery of an attitude to nature as sacred is 'not possible'. In what sense am I using that phrase? First, I want to suggest that it is not *morally* possible. Given what we know about the workings of nature, it would be *irresponsible* not to use that knowledge. It gives us the power to change things, and if we can use that power to reverse damaging changes to the natural world and to restore a better state of affairs, we have a responsibility to do so. There is also a second, and deeper, sense in which the attitude to nature as sacred is 'not possible'. Given the knowledge we have of the natural world and the power that it gives us, our relationship with nature just *is*, inescapably, different from what it once was. The idea of nature as sacred goes with a view of it as mysterious and opaque – as something which transcends our comprehension. There may be some sense in which we can take that view, but we cannot do so in the manner of our pre-scientific ancestors, for whom nature really was mysterious and incomprehensible. We know too much. We know, to a great degree, how to control nature, and where we cannot do so, we know in principle how to find out what we need to do in order to control it more effectively. We cannot divest ourselves of that knowledge, and the relationship with nature which it establishes is in the end incompatible with the recovery of a sense of the sacred.

I want now to raise a problem for my claim that we cannot revive the idea of nature as sacred, by returning to my use of Dworkin. I said that what he is most concerned to do is to articulate the idea of *human life* as sacred. Prince Charles's talk also includes that dimension. He says that 'we need to rediscover . . . a sense of the sacred in our dealings with the natural world, *and with each other*' (my emphasis). The 'technical fixes' which he distrusts include not only 're-engineering nature' but also 'redesigning humanity', and he warns against seeking 'to reduce the natural world *including ourselves* to the level of nothing more than a mechanical process' (my emphasis).[4] Does my argument apply here too? If I am claiming that a sense of the sacred is irrecoverable, does that commit me also to the claim that we can no longer regard human life as sacred? That would be worrying, and yet the same argument might seem to apply. We have the knowledge. We have the power. We know how to apply scientific knowledge and causal understanding in order to manipulate other human beings to achieve particular purposes. Does that mean that we can no longer acknowledge any barriers to our doing so? Is nothing inviolable?

That is not a conclusion which I wish to draw. I suggest that there is a difference between holding the natural world as sacred and holding other human lives as sacred. In the latter case, what sets limits to what is permissible is the *agency* of other human beings. Each of us is an independent agent, a being with experiences and projects of his or her own, and in our dealings with one another the agency of each of us is limited by the agency of others. It is this that imposes the boundaries, that sets up barriers against the instrumental use of other human lives.

That is a typically Kantian way of putting it, drawing on Kant's famous principle that we should treat human beings never solely as means but always also as ends in themselves.[5] Such a vocabulary is not the language of 'the sacred', and in my view it is more appropriate to what we should want to say here. The Kantian idea of 'respect for persons', or indeed of 'respect for human lives', captures more clearly the contrast which Dworkin wants to make between that way of valuing things and the idea of incremental value, and it might well have been more suited to Dworkin's discussion of the ethics of abortion and infanticide than is the idea of the sacred.

Let us now reverse the comparison between attitudes to nature and attitudes to human beings. Can this attitude of 'respect' be an appropriate way of characterising also our relationship with the natural world? I do not think that it can. Our actions towards other human beings are limited by their own agency, but our actions towards nature are not limited in the same way, because nature is not an agent in the same sense. Such an attitude may, perhaps, be appropriate towards at least some other non-human living things, but if it is, then it is appropriate just to the degree that we can see these other living things as capable of agency, and as having experiences and purposes which set moral limits to our own actions. It is a matter for philosophical debate how far we can appropriately see non-human animals in this way, but at least to some degree it may be appropriate. Respect understood in these terms is not, on the other hand, an attitude we can take towards natural species. Individual non-human living things may perhaps count as agents in the relevant sense, but species do not. Hence when Dworkin talks about natural species as another example of something which is sacred, I am not sure what to make of this. We cannot, at any rate, gloss it in the way in which I have wanted to gloss the idea of human lives as sacred. And if the attitude of respect is not appropriate to natural species, then by the same token it is not an appropriate response to nature as a whole. Unless we are going to personify Nature as an active force with its own plans and purposes, we cannot attribute to it that capacity for purposive agency which makes it a proper object of respect.

## Purposes in Nature

I have said that we cannot attribute purposive agency to nature. That assumption, however, can be questioned, for there is a long tradition of seeing nature in something like that way – the 'teleological' conception of nature which explains why natural things and processes are as they are by citing their 'final causes', the purposes which they serve. Here we have another, and different, contrast with the instrumental relationship to nature. The idea is not so much that nature is sacred and inviolable, but that if there are purposes in nature, these are purposes which we ought to respect and which set limits to and constraints on our use of nature for our own purposes.

The teleological conception of nature was given its classic formulation by Aristotle and has been central to much of the tradition of Christian thought.[6] Explanation in terms of the purpose or goal which is aimed at is most plausible when used to explain the structure and behaviour of living organisms. Plants have roots to draw up moisture from the soil; the spider spins its web to trap its prey; human beings have sharp front teeth for biting and flat back teeth for chewing – these are, for Aristotle, some of the myriad instances of purposive organisation in the natural world. Purposes in such cases are not necessarily conscious purposes. The plant is not aware of the purpose which its roots serve, nor do we humans consciously choose the shape of our teeth to serve their appropriate purposes. Rather, these purposes are simply 'built into' the workings of nature. Because purposes need not be conscious purposes, Aristotle is able to extend purposive explanation to non-living things. The four elements – earth, water, air and fire – each have, he thinks, their natural position in the universe, and their natural movement is therefore purposive movement, movement towards their natural position in the universe, with earth at the base, water above the earth, air above that, and fire uppermost. The scheme has undoubted explanatory power – this is why stones sink in water and bubbles of air rise to the surface of the water, why rain falls and fire leaps upwards.

The decisive philosophical attack on Aristotelian 'final causes' was

made by seventeenth-century philosophers such as Descartes and
Spinoza. They argue that we should not assume parochially that everything in nature has been created as it is for the benefit of human beings,
and we should not be so presumptuous as to suppose that we can know
God's mind and understand his purposes. Descartes says:

> it would be the height of presumption if we were to imagine
> that all things were created by God for our benefit alone, or
> even to suppose that the power of our minds can grasp the
> ends which he set before himself in creating the universe.[7]

These are bad reasons for rejecting Aristotelian final causes. For Aristotle, final causes are not to be found by trying to read God's mind, still
less by supposing that God made everything for our benefit. God does
play a role in the Aristotelian teleological world-picture, but it is not
that of a creator-god consciously shaping the natural world so that
everything serves its proper purpose and can be seen as beneficial from
a human point of view. That version of the teleological picture may be
closer to the Christian one, but it is not the only version of the idea of
purposes in nature. Descartes's reasons for rejecting final causes may
hold good against a crude Christian version of the idea, but they are not
good objections to final causes as such, and they do not adequately
explain the decisive turn against final causes. They therefore leave us
asking what was really going on in the seventeenth-century intellectual
revolution which replaced the teleological conception of the natural
world with the mechanistic conception.

Clearly that revolution was not only a philosophical revolution but
also a scientific revolution, and we might therefore be tempted to suppose that the former was merely a reflection of the latter and that
the change of philosophical world-view was driven by the scientific

discovery that the real explanations of natural phenomena were mechanistic explanations rather than teleological ones. That, however, would be equally unsatisfactory, for the change was not an empirical discovery – it was not as though scientists suddenly discovered that phenomena had mechanistic explanations. Rather it was a change in the understanding of what counted as a genuine explanation. It was a classic example of a paradigm shift – the replacement of one model by a different model governing scientific investigation. The new mechanistic paradigm proved scientifically more fruitful; it successfully generated new hypotheses and discoveries, and a huge quantity of detailed scientific work has now been built on it, to the point where it cannot be abandoned. The Aristotelian teleological world-view was a perfectly coherent one; it was a possible way of making sense of experience. It was indeed, as elaborated by Aristotle himself, a magnificent conceptual synthesis, and it has not been empirically refuted. It's just that it no longer underpins detailed scientific research and our detailed understanding of the physical world.

The weakest point in the Aristotelian scheme was its model for the explanation of the behaviour of inanimate bodies – the idea that each of the four elements tends towards its natural position. I have said that this model can explain much of our everyday experience. The greatest difficulty for Aristotelian physics, however, was that of explaining constrained motion, such as the behaviour of projectiles. When we throw a stone, why does it continue moving in the same direction as the movement of the hand? So long as it is actually in the hand, there is no explanatory problem – we explain its movement in terms of the purposes of the human agent who holds it. But when it leaves the hand, why doesn't its natural end-directed motion immediately take over? Why does it not start moving straight away towards its natural position? Medieval thinkers working within the Aristotelian tradition had developed quite sophisticated theories to explain the movement of projectiles in a way consistent with the Aristotelian idea of natural motion. Descartes's mechanistic view of the world, in contrast, does not start with the idea of end-directed natural motion and then try to fit projectiles into the picture; instead he starts with the motion of projectiles as the paradigm of motion and of his 'first law of nature', the law of inertia. He formulates this law as follows: 'Each and every thing, in so far as it can, always continues in the same state; and thus what is once in motion always continues to move.'[8] He immediately proceeds to illustrate this law with the case of projectiles:

> our everyday experience of projectiles completely confirms this first rule of ours. For there is no other reason why a projectile should persist in motion for some time after it leaves the hand that throws it, except that what is once in motion continues to move until it is slowed down by bodies that are in the way.[9]

What Descartes is in effect doing is formulating a view of the physical world in which constrained motion, instead of being the problem case, becomes the central case and provides the model for the explanation of all movement. This new paradigm cannot in any simple way be empirically shown to be correct, or the Aristotelian view false – as I have mentioned, the Aristotelian view had ways of accounting for constrained motion. The new paradigm, however, turns out to have vastly greater explanatory power. In Descartes's law of inertia we can recognise the precursor of Newton's first law of motion, and the starting-point of classical mechanics.

The relevance of the explanatory power of mechanistic explanations is apparent if we look at their application to the structure and functioning of the bodies of living things. This is where the teleological picture has its greatest intuitive appeal. It seems just obvious that teeth are as they are because they are for biting and chewing, that lungs are for breathing, and so on. The point was made forcibly by Descartes's contemporary, the Cambridge Platonist philosopher Ralph Cudworth:

> For is it not altogether as absurd and ridiculous, for men to undertake to give an account of the formation and organization of the bodies of animals, by mere fortuitous mechanism, without any final or intending causality, as why there was a heart here, and brains there; and why the heart had so many and such different valves in the entrance and outlet of its ventricles; and why all the other organic parts, veins and arteries, nerves and muscles, bones and cartilages, with the joints and members, were of such a form.[10]

The example of the workings of the heart is the very same example which Descartes discusses at length in a famous passage in Part V of his *Discourse on Method*, where he describes the operation of the valves by which the heart pumps blood around the body and offers this as a paradigm example of the power of mechanical explanations. 'This movement', he says, 'follows just as necessarily as the movement of a clock follows from the force, position, and shape of its counterweights and wheels'.[11] Descartes's ability to provide such an account does not by itself refute the teleological explanation framed in terms of the purpose of the heart. Why then does Descartes reject Cudworth's insistence on the indispensability of such an explanation? It would seem that he is simply not interested. He does not need to argue against the claim that the purpose of the heart is to pump the blood, he simply appears to ignore it as unilluminating, whereas the mechanical explanation provides immense scope for further investigation, and brings the particular case within a world-view in which essentially the same kind of explanation can be applied to innumerable other phenomena.

What I want to say about final causes and the teleological view of nature, then, is essentially similar to what I said about the 'sense of the sacred'. It is a possible attitude to nature, but it is not really a possible one for us now. The growth of scientific knowledge has changed our relationship with nature. That relationship is inescapably mechanistic in the broad sense that we have come to understand nature by understanding how to manipulate it and how to calculate and predict the consequences of natural causes. To the extent that the teleological view is a rival to the mechanistic view, we cannot turn back from the latter to the former without jettisoning the conceptual underpinning of our vastly extensive detailed knowledge of the natural world.

## Aesthetic Values in Nature

I have considered two possible alternatives to the instrumental view of nature – the idea of nature as sacred, and the idea of purpose in nature. I have argued that neither of these is a viable alternative to the instrumental view. Neither of them is an appropriate way of establishing limits to our use of nature for our own purposes. I have suggested that there is a sense in which neither is a possible view for us now, given the knowledge which we have of nature and the relationship which this establishes between us and the natural world.

Some might find this a disturbing conclusion. Echoing Prince Charles's concerns, they might say that if we regard it as acceptable for us to use nature simply for our own purposes, then there is nothing to stop us continuing to exploit it and destroy it as we have been doing. In response we should note first that the appeal to instrumental values may still impose firm limits on what we can do to nature. If we want to use the soil to grow crops and feed ourselves, we shall want to avoid over-exploiting it, eroding it and making it unusable in the long term. If we want to preserve human habitations, we shall be concerned that global warming may lead to a rise in the sea level and to widespread and devastating flooding and we shall need to work out how to prevent this. If we want to go on enjoying the countryside as a place of peace and tranquillity, we shall need to set some limit to the building of roads and the spread of cities. But still, it may be said, this is not enough; these concerns are symptoms of a deeper malaise, a reminder that we need to respect nature for its own sake. At this point some environmental philosophers are likely to talk of the need to recog-nise 'intrinsic values' in nature. The contrast is with instrumental value, and the suggestion is that nature, or certain components of the natural world, such as species or landscapes or natural habitats or eco-systems or biotic communities, have value in their own right and for their own sake, not just as means to satisfy human needs and desires.

Though talk of 'intrinsic value' is a standard piece of philosophical vocabulary, I find it unhelpful. The contrast with instrumental value is clear enough as far as it goes, but it does not take us very far. What does it mean to say that something has value 'in itself' or 'for its own sake'? Here is a classic formulation from a philosopher who was influential in giving the idea its currency. According to G. E. Moore, in order to answer the question 'What things have intrinsic value?', 'it is necessary to consider what things are such that, if they existed *by themselves*, in absolute isolation, we should yet judge their existence to be good'.[12] I want to retort that if intrinsic value is defined thus, then nothing has intrinsic value. Value is holistic. Things have value in virtue of the role which they play in our lives and the place which they occupy in our experience of the world. This does not reduce all value to instrumental value, but it does mean that value is essentially *relational*. Therefore, if we want to talk about non-instrumental values in nature, we still have to say more about why they are valuable, and to do so by explaining their significance within our experience as a whole and their relation to other features of our lives.

I want to suggest that the most plausible account of intrinsic value in nature (in the minimal sense of 'non-instrumental value') is an account of it as *aesthetic* value. To many environmentalists that suggestion seems too superficial, reducing nature simply to an object for our aesthetic enjoyment, something which we value simply for its beauty. That, they might say, is not an attitude of respect for nature as such, it is just another form of instrumental value. Is that right? Well, it depends of course on what account we give of aesthetic value, and we should first note that, as is generally recognised in philosophical aesthetics, there is much more to aesthetic value than just beauty. For a start there is the classic distinction, made by Kant among others, between aesthetic experience of the *beautiful* and of the *sublime*. Here are some examples Kant offers of our experience of the sublime:

> Bold, overhanging and . . . threatening rocks, thunder-clouds piled up the vault of heaven, borne along with flashes and peals, volcanoes in all their violence of destruction, hurricanes leaving desolation in their track, the boundless ocean rising with rebellious force, the high waterfall of some mighty river, and the like, make our power of resistance of trifling moment in comparison with their might.[13]

Kant has an unconvincing psychological account of why we value the sublime. He continues:

> But, provided our own position is secure, their aspect is all the more attractive for its fearfulness; and we readily call these objects sublime, because they raise the forces of the soul above the height of vulgar commonplace, and discover within us a power of resistance of quite another kind, which gives us courage to be able to measure ourselves against the seeming omnipotence of nature.[14]

Here the idea seems to be that though we find terrifying such features of nature as storms and volcanoes and mighty waterfalls and the boundless ocean, by viewing them aesthetically we can take delight in our ability to rise above that fear. This psychological explanation, however, is redundant; it adds nothing to the idea of the sublime. Simply drawing attention to the fearful and impressive character of such natural phenomena is sufficient to explain how and why we appreciate them aesthetically. What we appreciate and value is their *expressive* character.

Once we introduce the idea of the sublime as an object of aesthetic appreciation distinct from the idea of beauty, the way is open for us to recognise a whole range of other aesthetic objects and aesthetic values in nature, all of which are instances of what I want to describe as *expressive values*. Just as what we find aesthetically valuable in the arts is not at all confined to the appreciation of beauty, and an important dimension of it is the expressive character of works of art, so likewise the aesthetic value we find in nature is at least partly a matter of expressive value. The bleakness of a barren wilderness, the awesome majesty of a mountain peak, the starkness of the cliffs, the relentless power of the crashing waves – their value consists precisely in their bleakness, their awesome character, their starkness, their relentless power. These are features of nature which all contribute to the meaning the world has for us, they are all essential features of the sense we make of our experience. In that way they enrich our lives, not necessarily because they are beautiful, but because they are emotionally evocative. This is not instrumental value. It is not that we first have an independently identifiable need to find some things expressive, and then light upon features of nature as means of satisfying that need. Rather, these features of nature just are part of the world we have to make sense of; we find them powerfully expressive in these ways, and given that we do so, our experience would be diminished if they were to be destroyed.

I want to take three literary examples to illustrate the idea of expressive values in nature. Consider first a famous passage in Wordsworth's *Prelude* in which he describes his experience, when a boy, of rowing across a lake on a moonlit summer night:

> With an unswerving line, I fixed my view
> Upon the summit of a craggy ridge,
> The horizon's utmost boundary; far above
> Was nothing but the stars and the grey sky.
> She was an elfin pinnace; lustily
> I dipped my oars into the silent lake,
> And, as I rose upon the stroke, my boat
> Went heaving through the water like a swan;
> When, from behind that craggy steep till then
> The horizon's bound, a huge peak, black and huge,
> As if with voluntary power instinct
> Upreared its head. I struck and struck again,
> And growing still in stature the grim shape

Towered up between me and the stars, and still,
For so it seemed, with purpose of its own
And measured motion like a living thing,
Strode after me. With trembling oars I turned,
And through the silent water stole my way
Back to the covert of the willow tree;
There in her mooring-place I left my bark, –
And through the meadows homeward went, in grave
And serious mood . . .[15]

The young Wordsworth's feeling of being awed by the grim and men-acing crag is not an experience of beauty, nor an enjoyable experience, but it is one of immense significance for him.

Consider now another, fictional, example of a formative emotional experience defined in part by certain features of the natural world – the opening pages of Dickens's *Great Expectations*:

Ours was the marsh country, down by the river, within, as the river wound, twenty miles of the sea. My first most vivid and broad impression of the identity of things, seems to me to have been gained on a memorable raw afternoon towards evening. At such time I found out for certain, that this bleak place overgrown with nettles was the churchyard; and that Philip Pirrip, late of this parish, and also Georgina wife of the above, were dead and buried; and that Alexander, Bar-tholomew, Abraham, Tobias, and Roger, infant children of the aforesaid, were also dead and buried; and that the dark flat wilderness beyond the churchyard, intersected with dykes and mounds and gates, with scattered cattle feeding on it, was the marshes; and that the low leaden line beyond,

> was the river; and that the distant savage lair from which
> the wind was rushing, was the sea; and that the small
> bundle of shivers growing afraid of it all and beginning to
> cry, was Pip.[16]

The bleakness of the marshes is certainly not beautiful, nor would it be plausible to say that experiences of bereavement and loneliness and desolation have a valuable place in our experience. But given that such experiences are a part of the human condition, natural landscapes which are an objectified embodiment of the bleakness of certain aspects of our lives do have a value for us.

My third example, from Hardy's *The Return of the Native*, explicitly invokes the contrast between beauty and sublimity:

> Twilight combined with the scenery of Egdon Heath to
> evolve a thing majestic without severity, impressive without
> showiness, emphatic in its admonitions, grand in its sim-
> plicity. The qualifications which frequently invest the façade
> of a prison with far more dignity than is found in the façade
> of a palace double its size lent to this heath a sublimity in
> which spots renowned for beauty of the accepted kind are
> utterly wanting. Fair prospects wed happily with fair times;
> but alas, if times be not fair! Men have oftener suffered from
> the mockery of a place too smiling for their reason than
> from the oppression of surroundings oversadly tinged.
> Haggard Egdon appealed to a subtler and scarcer instinct,
> to a more recently learnt emotion, than that which responds
> to the sort of beauty called charming and fair.[17]

For all Hardy's over-insistent pessimism, he accurately captures our appreciation of aspects of nature which express a variety of human emotions, and our need for them because of these expressive qualities.

All these passages help to explain how we can value a wilderness not because it is beautiful but just because it is a wilderness, how we can value a menacing crag just because it is menacing and a barren heath just because of its barrenness. These are examples of what I mean by aesthetic values in nature. I want to stress again that there are perfectly good instrumental reasons why we should want to prevent the destruction of nature. However, we also rightly feel that those instrumental reasons are not the whole story, and in so far as there is another dimension to what we value in nature and want not to destroy, I suggest that it is more satisfactorily accounted for in terms of expressive values of this kind than by invoking a 'sense of the sacred'.

## Notes

1 The lecture, *Respect for the Earth – A Royal View and Conclusion*, can be found at http://www.nssd.net/references/Reith2000/reith6.htm. The quotation is from the third and fourth paragraphs.

2 Ibid., sixteenth paragraph.

3 Ronald Dworkin, *Life's Dominion* (HarperCollins paperback edition, London, 1995), chapter 3, pp. 68–84.

4 *Respect for the Earth*, third, fifteenth and sixth paragraphs.

5 Immanuel Kant, *Fundamental Principles of the Metaphysic of Morals* (also translated under other titles, such as *Groundwork of the Metaphysics of Morals*), second section. There are various English translations; see for example the 'Library of Liberal Arts' edition, translated by T. K. Abbott (Bobbs-Merrill, Indianapolis, 1949), pp. 45–46.

6 Aristotle, *Physics*, Book II, especially chapter 8.

7 René Descartes, *Principles of Philosophy*, III.2 (first published 1644), in *The Philosophical Writings of Descartes*, vol. 1, translated by John Cottingham,

Robert Stoothoff and Dugald Murdoch (Cambridge University Press, Cambridge, 1985), p. 248.

8  *Principles* II.37, in ibid., p. 240.

9  *Principles* II.38, in ibid., p. 241.

10 Ralph Cudworth, *The True Intellectual System of the Universe*, Book I, Ch. III, Section XXXVII, in *The Cambridge Platonists*, ed. Gerald R Cragg (Oxford University Press, New York, 1968), pp. 237f, and in *The Cambridge Platonists*, ed. C. A. Patrides (Edward Arnold, London, 1969), p. 291.

11 Descartes, *Discourse on Method*, Part V, in *The Philosophical Writings of Descartes*, p. 136.

12 G. E. Moore, *Principia Ethica* (Cambridge University Press, Cambridge, 1903), Ch. VI, Section 112.

13 Immanuel Kant, *The Critique of Judgement* (first published 1790, translated by J. C. Meredith, Oxford, 1952), First Part, 'Critique of Aesthetic Judgement', Section 28, p. 110.

14 Ibid., pp. 110–111.

15 William Wordsworth, *The Prelude*, 1850 version, lines 369–90 (Penguin Classics edition, Harmondsworth, 1995, p. 59).

16 Charles Dickens, *Great Expectations*, ch. 1 (Oxford University Press 'World's Classics' edition, Oxford, 1994, pp. 3–4).

17 Thomas Hardy, *The Return of the Native*, Book One, Ch. 1 (Macmillan 'New Wessex Edition', London, 1974, p. 34).

# 2   Is Nature Sacred?

## Response to Richard Norman

## Alan Holland

## Introduction

As commonly understood, use of the term 'sacred' implies a religious point of view, and perhaps a commitment to the existence of some divine or supernatural being. But I take it that we are not here debating whether or not nature is sacred in *that* sense. The answer would depend largely, and simply, on whether or not we were prepared to view the natural world as 'God's handiwork': it would quickly reduce, in other words, to yet another debate about the existence of God.

We are concerned, rather, with the possible application to nature of a secular notion that, on the one hand, retains the essential gravity of the religious notion but, on the other hand, avoids the associated metaphysical conviction. One motive for being interested in such an application is the need that many feel to step outside the range of secular concepts currently on offer, in order to express what it is that they find important about the natural world, without also having to step outside the realm of natural explanation.

Already, we can see two ways in which the proposal to ascribe sacredness to nature might be challenged. One way is to insist that no such notion of the sacred is available – that the metaphysical conviction is at the heart of what it means to be sacred, and cannot be detached from it. The other is to say that, even if it is available, it cannot be applied to nature. I interpret Richard Norman's view, which we shall discuss in due course, as tending towards this latter position. He does not deny the possibility of such a notion. Indeed, he seems prepared to apply it to human life. He insists, however, that there is no bridge from this admission to the sacredness of nature.

The former challenge raises far more issues than it is possible to tackle here. One pressing question, for example, would be how far there could be the same grounds for respect, the same proscription against certain sorts of human meddling with the natural order, once belief in a providential being had been abandoned. For present purposes, however, we shall adopt the working hypothesis that such a notion of the sacred is, or at least might be, available. This approach is not unreasonable if we reflect that reverence for the natural world did not necessarily wait upon the belief in a creator, but may in fact have preceded it. Historically speaking, the natural world has constantly struck people as what a being such as God *might* have created. And logically speaking, the character of the creation has often been presented as an overwhelming reason to believe in a creator. These facts suggest that although the character of the natural world as something it is appropriate to revere might be proffered as a *basis* for some form of religious belief, it does not necessarily presuppose it.

In what follows, I shall first offer some critical reflections on the case that Richard Norman presents against ascribing sacredness to nature, and then develop a positive case for the sacredness of nature that rests on challenging at least some of the assumptions that lie behind Norman's negative verdict.

## The Meaning of 'Sacred'

In developing his account of the term 'sacred', Norman first marks the connection between viewing something as sacred and viewing it non-instrumentally. He then refers with approval to Ronald Dworkin's suggestion that the sacred can be explained in terms of the concept of 'violation'. In Dworkin's view, to regard something as sacred is to regard it as something that we ought not, or may not, violate. 'It is this idea of "inviolability" that seems to me to be the key', says Norman, and continues: 'What is distinctive about "the sacred" is that it sets up boundaries or barriers which must not be crossed' (Norman 2004: 10). I do not demur from this suggestion, save to observe that while it might be true, normatively speaking, to say that the sacred ought not to be violated, what this implies, conceptually speaking, is that the sacred is precisely that which *can* be violated. And it is important, I believe, to be mindful of this distinction between normative and descriptive, since we might not all agree on the *behaviour* that it is appropriate to display towards what is sacred, even if we were to agree on what it means to be sacred. Hence, rather than describe the sacred as what must not (normatively speaking) be gainsaid, it is better, I suggest, to describe it, conceptually, as that whose gainsaying constitutes a violation (as opposed, say, to a miscalculation, an injury, or a mere wickedness).

The importance of the point can be illustrated by reference to Norman's claim that

> [t]o regard nature as sacred is to think of it as something on which we should not intrude. We should not apply our knowledge of nature and its causal laws simply in order to use it for human purposes.
>
> (Norman 2004: 10)

This claim is both normative and highly questionable. For one thing, those who view nature as God's handiwork can hardly be construed as proscribing 'intrusion', since bare survival would not otherwise be possible. For another, whilst conceptually it is true that to think of something as sacred is to think of it non-instrumentally, it surely does not follow that we are barred from using anything regarded as sacred instrumentally. This would seem, for example, to preclude someone's viewing their actions instrumentally as being performed 'for the glory of God'.

In addition, I would suggest that there are at least two further elements to be found within our concept of the sacred. One is that what is sacred is thought of as exempt from transactions of various kinds, not simply monetary transactions but perhaps 'trade-offs' of any kind. The other is that what is sacred demands a commitment that is unconditional – a commitment most famously exemplified by the readiness of Abraham to sacrifice Isaac, his son (Genesis XXII: vv. 1–14). Once again, these should be construed as conceptual, rather than normative points. Neither is meant to entail that the claim of the sacred is always and everywhere overriding. Hence, it is intended to allow for the fact that there may be occasions when it is morally defensible to give up something sacred. The force of saying that something *sacred* has been given up lies rather in what it would and would not be appropriate to say about such an event. It would perhaps, for example, rule out the question whether the transaction had or had not been 'fair'. Moreover, if we take our cue from how the term 'sacred' is understood in certain religious contexts, we find another sense in which 'violation' of the sacred is allowable. I am referring here to the concept of original sin – the notion that we cannot help but disappoint the godhead. Translated into the secular context, this would encourage a healthy recognition that some forms of 'violation' may be an inescapable concomitant of the human condition.

## Knowledge and Power

In light of his account of what it is to be sacred, Richard Norman argues that whereas it might once have been possible for us to view nature as sacred, we can now no longer do so '[g]iven the knowledge we have of the natural world and the power that it gives us' (Norman 2004: 11). The reasons he offers, then, are twofold. The first is: because we know too much. The second is: because, in light of this knowledge, our power over nature is too great.

The point about knowledge can be contested, initially, by register-ing a distinction between institutional and individual knowledge. The fact is that the bulk of current human knowledge is institutional, smeared out across a vast array of systems, rather than located at any particular point, and way beyond the reach of any individual to com-prehend. 'We' know how to fly to the moon, but this knowledge is not in the gift of any individual, nor indeed any group of individuals. The relevance of the point is that it is not some unidentifiable repository of institutional knowledge that may or may not be disposed to view nature as sacred, but individuals. And to press the point home, it might be argued that even though institutional knowledge may be at its 'high-est' level yet, and even perhaps *because* this is so, the resources that any given individual can call upon to cope unaided with the natural world are probably at their lowest level.

Nor should we overlook the fragility of knowledge. We can gain it, but we can also lose it. This applies as much to institutional as to individual knowledge, and it applies no matter how durable the ways we have found to 'store' knowledge. For, were we to lack the ability to interpret what has been stored, then what had been stored would no longer be knowledge. Historically, the haemorrhage of (classical) Greek and Roman wisdom is a case in point, and in more modern times, perhaps, the failure of the former Soviet Union to sustain its nuclear programme.

As a second response, I would contest Norman's claim that we can no longer view nature 'in the manner of our pre-scientific ancestors, for whom nature really was mysterious and incomprehensible' (p. 11). There is ample historical evidence for the awe and wonder that the natural world has inspired when conceived as the 'handiwork of God'. But many would agree with the sentiment expressed by Charles Darwin in the final paragraph of *The Origin of Species* that this response in no way diminishes when the supernatural explanation of how the natural world has arisen gives way to a naturalistic one (Darwin 1872: 401). Far from the sense of mystery and wonder belonging only to a pre-scientific viewpoint, it seems rather to be the source and inspiration for scientific endeavour itself.

To the point about power, I would also offer two rejoinders. The first is to repeat my earlier argument that to view nature as sacred, while it carries connotations of limits and constraints, cannot possibly entail our giving up all instrumental dealings with it. True, to ask how we can reduce carbon emissions or restore the quality of drinking water is not to think directly of nature as something sacred and inviolable. But at the same time, it doesn't obviously *preclude* such an attitude. Hence, I cannot accept Norman's claim that to think of nature as sacred would entail our relinquishing these projects.

But I also have a deeper concern, and this is with the very idea that 'we' now have such 'power over nature' that we cannot possibly recover our earlier, more reverential attitudes. It is not that I disagree with the claim, but that I fail to understand it. The intention, I assume, is to draw attention to the ways in which 'our' increased understanding of causal laws enables us to intervene more effectively to secure certain ends. Thus we (appear to) have more power over *our* lives. But I do not see how it follows that we thereby have more power over nature. If nature is sacred, then as instances of the sacred we can cite the song of the blackbird, or the spider's web glistening in the early morning dew. What I fail to understand is the claim that we have 'power' over the blackbird's song or the spider's web. The reason for this failure is beginning to emerge quite clearly, and will be a leading theme of my positive account: Richard Norman and I are understanding the term 'nature' in quite different ways.

With the next move in his argument, however, I have no quarrel. This is his section entitled 'Purposes in Nature' in which he argues against attributing purposive agency to nature. My only quarrel is with the presupposition of the section – that if there were purposes in nature then this might qualify nature to be sacred. On the contrary, I propose to argue that if there is sacredness in nature, it is because nature is devoid of purpose.

## The Aesthetic Turn

For his positive account, Richard Norman turns to the aesthetic perspective, where this is understood in a suitably enlarged sense to encompass our appreciation of a whole range of 'expressive' qualities to be found in nature, including such qualities as the bleak, the awe-inspiring, the relentless and the menacing. What Norman is out to capture is a non-instrumental view of nature, and this he certainly does: the 'uses' of a bleak terrain and relentless rain are limited; the only thing to do is endure them.

My first difficulty with the suggestion, however, is that I do not know whether I should be contesting it at all. This is due to an uncertainty about the scope of the expressive qualities to which Norman is drawing our attention. I note that they include the awe-inspiring, and that they 'contribute to the meaning the world has for us' (Norman 2004: 23). But both of these properties could quite properly be attributed to the sacred. In similar vein, when Bernard Williams speaks of 'Promethean fear' (the sense that nature will exact a terrible revenge if we fail to show it proper respect), and when David Wiggins appeals to the notion of 'holy dread', arguing that we do not need a religious perspective in order to make sense of such a response to nature, they appear to be identifying expressive qualities very close to sacredness (Williams 1992: 67; Wiggins 2000: 27). And William Wordsworth, whom Norman enlists in his cause, would have been hard pressed to draw a line between these 'aesthetic' expressive qualities and the intimation of deeper things that he sensed in the woods above Tintern Abbey (Wordsworth 1965: 163–165).

I do have another, more combative difficulty to raise. The nub of the point is that the aesthetic reading is inevitably partial. In Richard Norman's version we notice a focus on the sublime, including the bold, the barren and the bleak, rather than on the beautiful, which might have included the delicate, the dancing and the delirious. Either way we note the absence of the mundane, the miserable and the monotonous, which are to be found in nature in equal measure. Others focus on the dramatic and the spectacular, to the neglect of the trivial and unspectacular. But a defence of spectacular nature is not a defence of nature. As John Stuart Mill points out, albeit in a different context: 'If it is a sufficient reason for doing one thing, that nature does it, why not another thing? If not all things, why anything?' (Mill 1874: 18). Mill's message is clear. If we wish to make a general statement about nature, to the effect that it is sacred, or (as in the passage quoted) that we should use it as a guide to action, then we cannot pick and choose. If only some aspects of nature are sacred, then it is not nature that is sacred, but some other feature that only some aspects of nature possess. To ascribe sacredness to nature has to be an all or nothing matter, if we mean to speak of nature as such: if we try to find the sacred in nature by looking towards the spectacular and the sublime, we're looking in the wrong place. Now in the final analysis, it may turn out that this partial perspective is all that we can defend. I am simply pointing out that, because it lacks the relevant kind of universality, it won't do as a surrogate for the claim that *nature* is sacred.

## 'Ecography'

There is undoubtedly a tension that besets the attempt to juxtapose the terms 'nature' and 'sacred'. In seeking to apply the term 'sacred' to nature, we are borrowing from a domain (the supernatural) that is defined precisely in opposition to the domain (the natural) to which we seek to apply it. The claim that nature is sacred therefore requires us to identify features that confer 'heightened' status while remaining rooted in the natural domain. It also requires that these features attach to nature itself, and not simply to aspects of it (like 'sublime'). Where to start?

First, a metaphysical proposal. The proposal is that we should understand the term 'nature' in a very particular way. Not as referring to a set of causal laws, or to some cut-and-come-again 'system', but as referring to a unique and historically contingent biosphere delivered to us largely through the processes of natural selection. For the study of such an entity we might propose the label 'eco-graphy' as a complement to 'eco-logy', understood (after Haeckel) as the study of the conditions under which natural selection occurs. In other words 'nature' is to be construed, in the way that Saul Kripke suggests we construe terms for natural kinds, as a 'rigid designator', or name, of an individual (Kripke 1980: 3–15, 48). On this reading, 'nature' would not refer to whatever could *possibly* come about by natural processes, but exclusively – and therefore 'rigidly' – to the particular historical nature that has *actually* come about. It means our thinking of natural selection not in terms of the inevitable march of progress nor as a system designed to produce 'winners'. It means our thinking of it instead as a quite fragile process of historical stumbling that happens to have produced a biosphere, but so easily might not have done: in short, as something miraculous.

An increasing number of contemporary evolutionary biologists view species, logically speaking, in a similar light (Hull 1978; Mayr 1987). According to this phylogenetic, or 'cladist' view, a species is a particular spatio-temporal population of organisms that falls between two speciation 'events'. And the very same kinds of conceptual grounds that are used to support the contention that species are one-off individuals rather than recurring types or classes – for example, that they have a beginning (and end) in time and can become extinct – would also support the contention that the nature that they help to constitute is also a particular and unique phenomenon rather than a (repeatable) kind. Furthermore, this view would help explain concerns about 'irreversibilities', and about the 'loss' of biodiversity; for these concerns seem to presuppose a conception of the natural world as a unique rather than a recurring phenomenon. Finally, there is a striking parallel between the basis of the case for sacredness in nature being proposed here, and the basis of the case for sacredness in art put forward elsewhere in this volume by Matthew Kieran – namely that it constitutes what Kieran described, at the conference on which this volume is based, as an 'unrepeatable generative achievement'.

## Nature and the Conditions of Life

Understood in this way, we can begin to see how nature might qualify for special status. Essentially the idea is that we look for the sacredness of nature not in any properties that it has but in the relation that obtains between nature, life, and human life in particular. Nature is not simply a necessary condition for life, but a pre-condition, and a pre-condition of *our* life. The relation between humans and the biosphere mirrors the relation between a human individual and their parents. It is the necessary originating source of human life. This pre-conditional status helps to explain why it might present us with the demands mentioned earlier as (a) unconditional, and (b) brooking no transaction. There can be no transaction between something that is a pre-condition and that for which it is the pre-condition, because we can bring no proportionality or commensuration to bear on the situation. For a similar reason the demand that nature presents us with has to be without conditions, or – which is the same thing – unconditional. Corresponding 'violations' occur when we cross this boundary and treat the pre-conditional as conditioned, e.g. as subject to transaction.

A similar conclusion follows from reflecting on the question of whether nature can be said to have 'intrinsic value'. For this notion, far from clarifying what it means to be sacred both seriously misrepresents it, and appears in fact to be a deeply unstable notion. The intuition behind the idea that there is *intrinsic* value in nature is that nature itself is a measure or yardstick of value. However, the force behind the notion that nature has intrinsic *value* is that nature is open to human judgement: at any rate, it is hard to construe the concept of value as anything other than the (possible) issue of human judgement. So, the implication of the claim that nature has value – intrinsic or otherwise – is that humans are in a position to *stand in judgement on* nature. But this is surely an absurd conceit. The natural world, one wants to say, is beyond judgement because it is itself a precondition of any judgement – and therefore of value – and a precondition indeed of any human enterprise.

In his discussion of happiness in the *Nicomachean Ethics*, Aristotle makes a useful and relevant distinction between what it is appropriate to *praise*, and what it is appropriate to *prize*. We praise virtue, he says, but should prize happiness because it is 'greater and better'. Of particular interest is the reason that he gives. One should prize rather than praise happiness (or blessedness) because it is 'godlike', and it is absurd to 'praise' the gods: 'for we never praise happiness as we praise justice, but we count it blessed, as something better and more godlike' (Aristotle 1999: 1101b26–27). In terms of Aristotle's distinction, my contention is that the natural world is to be prized rather than praised (or found wanting). It is just as absurd to praise (or value) the natural world as it would be to praise (or value) god. There is the same massive failure of a sense of proportion.

## Living with the Sacred

To regard nature as sacred, I claim, gets something right about our relationship to the natural world. But too often discussion stops at this point. As if the establishment of its sacred quality would immediately guarantee respect for nature. But arguably, it has precisely the opposite effect.

The first reason is Mill's – that nature is amoral. As he famously observes: 'In sober truth, nearly all the things which men are hanged or imprisoned for doing to one another are nature's everyday performances' (Mill 1874: 17). There is no immediately obvious conflict, in other words, between the claim that nature is sacred, and the claim that it is amoral. But this should really come as no surprise if we recall the religious model, and Abraham's readiness to sacrifice his son. The truth is that there is a permanent possibility of conflict between the demands of the sacred and the demands of the ethical. Both kinds of demand are frequently represented as having an absolute and overriding priority; but this seems to be a mistake, as Kaebnick also argues (2000: 22). What is true of each is not that they silence all other demands, but rather that they cannot be silenced – that their overriding comes at a cost. The only real question here is how far this depiction of conflict between the ethical and the sacred is an accurate reflection of the human condition, which I contend that it is.

The second reason reaches back to the age of Greek tragedy, when the Sophoclean chorus in *Antigone* first sang of the wonders of humankind. Since that time, one could argue, the inclination towards obeisance and worship associated with a recognition of the sacred has been in decline. Hence it is neither knowledge nor power that makes it impossible for us to view nature as sacred, but the rise of humanism. However, it is far from obvious that obeisance is the only, or even the appropriate, response to the sacred. Just as, in religious terms, it is possible to be quite mature about original sin, so it is possible to look (sacred) nature in the eye and not blink. In particular, to hold nature sacred does not in my view provide any support for the lamentable tendency of environmentalists to castigate humans for their stupidity, ignorance and greed – for their *abuse* of nature. Such condemnation comes easy, and no doubt many abusive practices have occurred in the course of human history. However, this diagnosis is a travesty of that history. Much of the human appropriation of environmental resources has been, and continues to be, a relatively innocent affair – ordinary people trying to scratch a living, stave off the elements, and feed themselves and their families. No violation of the sacred here – and no call to set humanism at odds with respect for nature.

I conclude that living with the sacred is far from an anomaly in contemporary life. In the final analysis, to hold out for the sacred, in any domain, is not to foster obedience, nor to castigate, nor even to bring comfort. It is much more about holding out for a deeper meaning to life, and holding out against banality.

## References

Aristotle (1999) *Nicomachean Ethics*, 2nd edn (tr. T. Irwin), Indianapolis: Hackett.

Darwin, C. (1872) *The Origin of Species*, 2nd edn, London: John Murray.

Dworkin, R. (1993) *Life's Dominion*, New York: Harper Collins.

Hull, D. (1978) 'A Matter of Individuality', *Philosophy of Science* 45: 335–360.

Kaebnick, G. (2000) 'On the Sanctity of Nature', *Hastings Center Report* 30, no. 5: 16–23.

Kieran, M. (2004) 'Is Art Sacred?', in B. Rogers (ed.) *Is Nothing Sacred?*, London: Routledge.

Kripke, S. (1980) *Naming and Necessity*, Oxford: Blackwell.

Mayr, E. (1987) 'The Ontological Status of Species', *Biology and Philosophy* 2: 145–166.

Mill, J. S. (1874) 'Nature', in *Three Essays on Religion*, London: Longman.

Norman, R. (2004) 'Nature, Science, and the Sacred', in B. Rogers (ed.) *Is Nothing Sacred?*, London: Routledge.

Wiggins, D. (2000) 'Nature, Respect for Nature and the Human Scale of Values', *Proceedings of the Aristotelian Society* 100: 1–32.

Williams, B. (1992) 'Must a Concern for the Environment be centred on Human Beings?', in C. C. W. Taylor (ed.) *Ethics and the Environment*, Oxford: Corpus Christi College: 60–68.

Wordsworth, W. (1965) *Poetical Works*, London: Oxford University Press.

# 3   Is Art Sacred?

## Nigel Warburton

The simple answer to the question 'Is Art Sacred?' is 'No'. Nothing is sacred, so art isn't. Remove God and the idea of the sacred becomes obsolete. The concept of the sacred is essentially dependent on religious and magical ways of thinking and is infused with religious connotations and assumptions. If something is sacred, then it is inviolable; its value is not instrumental but intrinsic; it is hallowed, and should be preserved at any cost. To call something sacred is to declare that it cannot be touched, damaged, destroyed, or even challenged or questioned. Why not? Because it emanates from God.

This style of thinking, of course, has its source in religious belief. But the tendency to treat things as sacred can remain long after the death of God has been acknowledged, distorting and infecting our evaluation of things. Here I want to sketch a number of the ways in which we tend to treat works of art – and in particular one-off original works of visual art such as paintings – as sacred.

First, I want to make it clear that the persisting attitudes I am discussing here are not attitudes towards the subject matter of religious paintings. Obviously many great works of art have what might be considered sacred subject matter. Produced in a religious age, there is no surprise that Leonardo's *Madonna of the Rocks* depicts a sacred (= 'once considered sacred') subject matter. But he (or she) who drives fat oxen is not necessarily fat: there is no reason why we should treat works of art with a religious subject matter as sacred once we have an enlightened view of religion. When I say that we tend to treat original works of art as sacred, then, I'm not suggesting anything about their subject matter.

## Are Works of Art Sacred Relics?

It is difficult to go into London's National Gallery or New York's Metropolitan Museum without being aware of the temple-like ambience. Even London's Tate Modern has turned a turbine hall into a cathedral interior. This sets the scene for a quasi-religious genius-worship, where the artist becomes a kind of god, or at least a saint, and the gallery-goer a worshipper. This is the 'bogus religiosity' that John Berger diagnosed in his *Ways of Seeing* (Berger 1972: 23). Queuing to see the recent Vermeer exhibition at the National Gallery, clutching guide notes like bibles, the art lovers surge forwards when the guard lets them in. There at last they stand in front of *Woman Pouring Milk* in (mostly) silent rapture. True, there is a certain amount of jostling from earnest art lovers, and there is a smeary bit of bullet-proof glass in front of the painting. But standing there I can't help feeling that I am enjoying a special kind of experience. This is, after all, not a copy, but the real thing, the very painting that Vermeer himself stood in front of. The great temptation is to treat this as an experience of a sacred relic.

What is a relic? In the religious context it is an object – a saint's bone, a piece of cloth worn by a prophet, a nail from the true cross. The object has had close contact with someone special, or perhaps was a part of him or her, and thereby acquired some kind of power in itself. The notion of a relic plays on precisely the magical thinking that James Frazer in *The Golden Bough* calls 'contagious magic'. Magic in general, according to Frazer, is 'a spurious system of natural law as well as a fallacious guide of conduct; it is a false science as well as an abortive art'. Contagious magic is essentially a misapplication of the association of ideas – making too much of contiguity. As Frazer puts it: 'contagious magic commits the mistake of assuming that things which have been in contact with each other are always in contact' (Frazer 1957: 15).

The original painting, as opposed to a facsimile, was in contact with the great Vermeer. And now as I stand in front of it I have a special kind of experience that I couldn't have in the presence of a mere facsimile, no matter how accurate a copy. Even if the facsimile were easier to view, because not behind glass, I feel that I would get something unique and almost inexpressible from being before the glass-covered original. This is much more than just the knowledge that this painting is in a causal chain that leads directly back to Vermeer himself: that alone could not justify the reverential feelings. This is the aura of the original art work that Walter Benjamin made so much of in his 'The Work of Art in the Age of Mechanical Reproduction' (Benjamin 1973). This aura was, according to Benjamin, supposed to wither as reproduction of images became more sophisticated. But it is not obvious that this has happened. My pilgrimage to the art gallery seems to have given me more than I could ever have got from a photographic reproduction of the paintings no matter how accurate they were (and despite their being just one or two links further down the causal chain from Vermeer's studio). Postcards, illustrations in books, slides, and so on all function as advertisements for the thing itself, the real Vermeer painting.

There may be non-magical explanations of this phenomenon. For example, the philosopher Nelson Goodman has suggested that a good reason for preferring original paintings over brilliant forgeries of them is that minute differences between paintings can have profound aesthetic significance (even if we are unaware of the precise causes of the differences of experience) – a point also made by Clive Bell. No matter how good the process of copying there is always the possibility that the copy will lack something that could later become visible to the sensitive viewer (Goodman 1976: 108).

Yet this can't explain a preference for all originals over copies. We can know for certain, for example, that some over-cleaned paintings lack many of the aesthetic qualities that an excellent copy of them in an earlier state will have. In such cases the aura of the original still exerts its force. So whilst we might concede that there are excellent reasons in many cases for preferring some original works to copies, this can't be the explanation in every case. Besides, Goodman's line of argument is only going to give us an intellectual account of why we should experience some original works; but the phenomenon I've described is to some extent an emotional, perhaps even visceral, one.

Another non-magical explanation of our experience of original art works is that knowledge that a painting is original and not a copy provides a spur to imaginative engagement with the work. It's not that we really believe we are put in touch with the artist through this encounter, but we play a little game of make believe that we are in touch in order to engage our imaginations. Without the jolt provided by this sort of encounter, the imagination may not be engaged. Perhaps this is what happens. Wittgenstein in his critical account of Frazer's *Golden Bough* suggested that Frazer was wrong to see magic as a kind of false science. Rather we should see it as an expressive and symbolic activity:

> Kissing the picture of one's beloved. That is obviously not based on the belief that it will have some specific effect on the object which the picture represents. It aims at

satisfaction and achieves it. Or rather it aims at nothing at
all; we just behave this way and then we feel satisfied.

(Wittgenstein 1993: 123)

Are we then just to say that 'we behave this way towards original
paintings and feel satisfied'? We treat them with a reverence and awe
that goes far beyond their appearances and is much closer to the attitude of the religious worshipper before a sacred relic. We don't really
believe that we are put in touch with the artist-god, but our actions are
expressive and symbolic. The frisson from the original work on this
account proceeds from make-believe. On this account we know at some
level that the real object cannot magically put us in touch with the artist
any better than can an excellent reproduction, but we persist in acting
as if it could. Yet the question remains: Why do we behave in this sort
of way?

Perhaps the frisson comes from our falling into magical ways of
thinking that are hardwired into us. Such patterns of thinking are not
easily overcome. Think of how we value objects that have been in touch
with people now dead over indistinguishable tokens of the same type: a
pen that belonged to a favourite uncle, or a grandmother's wedding
ring. The objects' particular histories do not usually leave their traces
on the objects; yet we treat them as if they have done. We speak of an
object's 'sentimental value'; but on what does such sentimental value
rely? Ultimately we seem just to have this preference for objects that
have actually played a particular causal role: we want to see the actual
paintings that Vermeer painted, not excellent copies of them. We want
the actual ring that our grandmother wore, and no other ring could
ever replace it. We are just like that. In the case of our experience of
original works of art as relics, though, we should be careful that this
preference for the original does not become worship of the original.

Original works of art are not sacred relics. At the most they are relics, and our experience of them is coloured by that fact. Perhaps in the future, once copying technologies have become sophisticated enough, we may eventually come to see works of visual art as types, not unique objects, with what we now see as the original as akin to a musical score of which there may be many performances some of which may be more interesting as works of art than the score itself.

## Do Works of Art have Intrinsic Value?

Another way in which quasi-religious attitudes may affect our experiences of art is in a temptation to see works of art as having intrinsic value, being valuable in themselves, independently of the experiences they might give rise to. The philosopher Ronald Dworkin in his book *Life's Dominion* maintains that many people treat great works of art as sacred in the sense that once created they have value independently of the act of viewing them:

> They are valuable, and must be respected and protected, because of their inherent quality as art, and not because people happen to enjoy looking at them or find instruction or some pleasurable aesthetic experience standing before them. We say that we want to look at one of Rembrandt's self-portraits because it is wonderful, not that it is wonderful because we want to look at it. The thought of its being destroyed horrifies us – seems to us a terrible desecration – but this is not just because or even if that would cheat us of experiences we desire to have. We are horrified even if we have only a very small chance of ever seeing the painting anyway – perhaps it is privately owned and never shown to

the public, or in a museum far away – and even if there are
plenty of excellent reproductions available.

(Dworkin 1993: 72).

But imagine a Vermeer painting locked in a vault with a device that destroys the painting if anyone opens the vault. Under these circumstances no one will ever see this painting again. If you believe that the work has intrinsic value you will surely believe that the world in which the painting continues to exist unseen is a better one than the one in which it is destroyed. Yet surely this is wrong. The only reason you might be tempted to take that line is that in most equivalent cases in real life there is, as long as the painting continues to exist, the faint chance that it might survive – that someone might find a way of defusing the destructive device. In the thought experiment no such chance exists.

Much of the impetus for talk of works of art having intrinsic value independent of our experience or possible experience of them, like similar talk of the intrinsic value of parts of nature, is a vestige of religious magic. Everything has value in God's eyes. And God sees things that even humans can't. The difference between the natural world case and the artistic one is that natural living things are parts of ecosystems, and destruction of any part of those systems potentially impacts on other parts and ultimately on sentient beings. So in most ecological cases there is an instrumental defence of why a particular habitat's destruction is wrong. In the case of works of art, their value lies not simply in their continuing existence, but in their potential to be appreciated. Their value then is not intrinsic. They are not sacred in that sense.

## Is the Category of Art Sacred?

A further way in which religious styles of thinking can colour our experience of art is in the way in which some people treat all art as sacred. The whole category of art, not just the subcategory of great works of art, is considered to have value simply because it is art. On this view the fact that something is a work of art makes it valuable. The philosopher George Dickie has tried to lay this odd belief to rest by stressing that the descriptive and evaluative senses of 'art' are separable: as he puts it, 'One can make a work of art out of a sow's ear, but that doesn't necessarily make it a silk purse' (Dickie 1997: 86). On this he is surely correct. To treat all works of art as inviolable would have absurd consequences on almost every definition of what art is. At the very least bad art should be immune from this reverential treatment.

## Conclusion

Great works of art are among the highest achievements of humanity. They are not, however, sacred. Original paintings are not sacred relics, though we might not be able to stop treating them as relics. They do not have intrinsic value: their value resides in their potential to be experienced. And the category of art is not itself sacred: to show that something is a work of art leaves open the question of whether or not we should accord it reverence. So art is not sacred in any obvious sense.

## References

Benjamin, W. (1973) 'The Work of Art in the Age of Mechanical Reproduction' in W. Benjamin, *Illuminations*, trans. H. Zohn, London: Collins, pp. 219–254.

Berger, J. (1972) *Ways of Seeing*, London: Penguin.

Dickie, G. (1997) *Introduction to Aesthetics*, Oxford: Oxford University Press.

Dworkin, R. (1993) *Life's Dominion*, London: Harper Collins.

Frazer, J.G. (1957) *The Golden Bough*, London: Macmillan.

Goodman, N. (1976) *Languages of Art*, 2nd edn, Indianapolis: Hackett.

Wittgenstein, L. (1993) 'Remarks on Frazer's *Golden Bough*' in *Philosophical Occasions 1912–1951*, ed. J. Klagge and A. Nordmann, Indianapolis: Hackett, pp. 115–155.

# 4   Art and the Limitations of Experience

## Matthew Kieran

### Introduction

The term sacred is shot through with religious resonance. Strictly speaking it means consecrated by God. So in one sense, devoid of religious belief, art can be anything but sacred. Yet we might have to appreciate art in a manner akin to the sacred. For art's value might not always be reducible to the value of the experience afforded.

Talk of art as sacred is somewhat precious and misleading. Consider the nature of religious icons. In the Roman Catholic tradition icons are sacred because they represent an ideal to be honoured and are aids to devotion. In these terms the artistry, originality or otherwise of an icon is beside the point. It was commonplace for icons and altar pieces created by superior artists to be repainted by journeymen. The original, or parts thereof, may have been lost but the icon still served its religious function. The Protestant destruction of icons and altar pieces was sacrilegious not because great works of art were destroyed, though that may be how we view it today, but because it constituted a profane violation of religious ideals and devotional aids. In secular terms, our attitude to the destruction of original works is rather different. It is the loss of the original artistry that we mourn. So perhaps a clue to art's value lies in examining why we value original works of art.

## Original Art Works

Why do we value original art works? Warburton suggests that it is the result of a religious hangover, a sense of mystery in which the art world clothes itself without rational justification. The artist is elevated to God-like status, the curators are the art world's priests and proselytisers, the galleries and museums its temples, and the art-going public are the laity kept at a worshipful distance. Warburton's thought is that divested of such mystery, the original will be found to have no special value. The challenge might be put like this: Given the virtues of the mass reproduction of art works, and their quality, what is the point in going to see originals? Now in the case of many visual art forms, such as painting, it is thought that the original makes a difference because the quality of the experience we will get is likely to be much better. No matter how good the reproduction, we are bound to see something in the original that we had missed in the reproduction. And the thought is fair enough. Colours, textures, tonal relations and scale often come out differently in reproductions. But now imagine we could guarantee a painterly reproduction which was indiscernible from the original. And imagine a museum filled to the brim with perfect replicas of the greatest paintings in the world. Why should we value the originals more then? Surely what matters is the quality of the experience afforded viewers – and the quality from the copy is the same as that we would get from the original.

Yet we value originals over and above the value of the experiences they afford (Davies 2003). Consider Leonardo da Vinci's *The Last Supper* (1495–1498), a wall painting in the refectory of the Santa Maria delle Grazie, Milan. The Last Supper was traditional subject matter for refectories. The originality of composition, drama and emotional impact was such that nothing quite like it had been seen before. It portrays the moment after Christ has just announced that one amongst them will betray him. The disciples are agitated, the four groupings structured into a whole by their gestures centring around a calm Christ amidst a maelstrom of confusion. Christ's arms are outstretched, his right hand reaches out to share a portion of bread with Judas, thus welcoming his fate, whilst his eyes are downcast towards his left hand in a gesture of sacrifice. Leonardo dispensed with the conventional halo, giving Christ luminosity from the landscape behind, and the shadowy overcast representation of Judas marks out his treachery.

Leonardo painted the work with an experimental mixture of tempera and oil which enabled him to achieve something close to the effect of oils, previously unheard of for a wall painting. But the nature of the mixture was such that most of the pigment didn't stick to the wall and it started to suffer from chronic deterioration soon after it was completed. Copies were, however, made. One of the best hangs in the Da Vinci Museum, Tongerio, Italy. Copied in the sixteenth century, it's almost as big as the original and possesses a wealth of detailing and colour that is no longer visible in Leonardo's wall painting (even after restoration). Now on Warburton's criteria it should be the case that we value the copy more than the original. The copy gives the viewer a richer, more complex, more striking visual experience than the original. But we don't. We value the original more. Why? Because the original is constitutive of Leonardo's achievement. It was Leonardo's painting as he did it, creating its unique compositional structure, transforming conventional imagery and humanising the scene, which constitutes the achievement. The other is a mere copy. The original is the genuine expression of a vision, attitude and conception of the Last Supper. It is the expression of a singular imagination. The copy apes its outward show.

Consider a different kind of case. Some of the earlier cubist works, such as Braque's *Bathing Woman* (1907–1908) and Picasso's *Portrait of Fernande* (1909), are not amongst the most visually dynamic, complex or interesting works of this movement. They don't rank, in terms of the value of the experience they afford, with some of the later cubist paintings. Yet we rate them highly – often more highly than later, more visually complex and rewarding but less original works. For these early creations were amongst the first to fragment visual planes in the multiplication of viewpoints so distinctive of the cubist style. It was with such works that the modernist breach from Cezanne first began.

## Valuing Art

The above considerations imply that there's something problematic about Warburton's conception of artistic value. He asks us to imagine a thought experiment. In a safe is a work we're led to believe is a masterpiece or, at least, by a master. Tragically the safe is wired up in such a way that if it is ever opened an explosion results, destroying both the safe and its contents. So we have a work which no-one can look at and appreciate. The question is, is the work of any value? Warburton suggests not, because the work can't be experienced. But it's far from clear this is the right inference at all, even for someone who holds that artistic value is a function of the value of our experience. Rather, we are unable to experience and appreciate something that is of value, which is why it would be a tragedy that the safe is so wired up.

Consider an ancient civilisation like that of the Aztecs. As the recent Royal Academy exhibition showed us, there are some wondrous artistic artefacts preserved from their culture. No doubt many more were destroyed and some of those, we imagine, would have been amongst the most beautiful objects that culture produced. Hernán

Cortés characterised the Aztec capital as 'the most beautiful thing in the world'; contemporary accounts from other conquistadors and fellow travellers agreed and Albrecht Dürer described collected treasures from there in glorious terms:

> All the days of my life I have seen nothing that touches my heart so much as these things, for I saw among them wonderful works of art, and I marvelled at the subtle *ingenia* of men in foreign lands ... Indeed, I cannot express my feelings about what I saw there.
>
> (Wood 2002: 38).

So we've every reason to believe that beautiful, impressive works were destroyed by the ravages of war, imperialism and history.

Presumably we consider it a loss that such objects were obliterated. For had those objects survived we would have been able to experience them and, hypothetically speaking, they would have been worth looking at. So too with the work in the safe. We don't know for sure how good the work in the safe really is. It could be a piece of artistic juvenilia rather than an artistic masterpiece. But, hypothetically, imagine it is a great work. If it is a great work, even on Warburton's criteria, it is structured in such a way that it would give viewers a worthwhile experience. So we can say that the work in the safe does possess artistic value. For it is artfully constructed in a way which would give someone, were they able to look at it, an aesthetically interesting and appealing experience. Even if value is reducible to experience, a world in which there are no people and only the remnants of great art or civilisations does possess value. For that world contains things that were they to be experienced would be found to be valuable.

There is something problematic about the way in which we've been encouraged to think about the value of art. Warburton's account looks as if it's an attempt to go one way in the face of a Euthyphro-type dilemma: either we appreciate a work for particular reasons, construed in terms of the properties of the experience the work gives the viewer, or it looks arbitrary. So Warburton opts for the first response. And then it looks as if we don't really value the work at all but the experience. So the art work itself looks eminently dispensable. Presumably anything that could provide the same kind of experience would be just as valuable.

Setting things up this way, however, is distorting. It's as if the quality of the experience can be severed from the work itself. But that can't be right. What it is for a work to be the work it is, must be constituted in terms of the essential properties it possesses, some of which will include the kind of experience it's disposed to afford. So to appreciate the experience afforded by a work just is, at least if it is being appreciated properly, to appreciate the work itself. We value the original works themselves, not just particular experiences they may happen to give us. This is why it is so crucial that we spend time, effort and patience in trying to get to grips with the essential nature of a work; what's really meant by the symbolism, the expressivity of the language, paint or compositional structure. Art works are not just vessels for experience. Conceiving of them as if they were would undercut much of our engagement with at least some great works. We often strive to perceive and experience a work aright, so we arrive at a correct understanding of the vision the artist is trying to get us to see.

A different way of getting at the same point is to consider the essentiality of origin. What this opaque phrase picks out is the idea that what matters regarding our attitudes to something are not just a function of what its inherent qualities are, but also a matter of the relations in which the object stands to other things. It's easier to grasp the point if we consider a concrete case. Imagine that there are a cluster of houses in a cul-de-sac which are all identical, but only one of them is the house your great-grandfather built. The rest are perfect imitations easily built by a modern construction firm last year. Should you treat all the houses in the same way, will your attitudes towards all of them be similar? If the only thing that mattered concerned how the houses looked, then the answer would be yes. But this is not the case. You have good reason to care about, and act differently toward, one of the houses in virtue of the fact that your grandfather built it and building such a house 100 years ago was a difficult thing to do. Similarly, there could be two paintings that are exactly the same in terms of appearance but the relations in which they stand both to each other and their origins may be different: one of them was created by the artist we credit with the work, the other was perfectly copied from that original by someone else. The copy may happen to give exactly the same rewarding experience that the original gives when you look at it (just as all the houses look alike). But it is nonetheless a copy of the original work. A work's origin can matter because whether it is an original may mark a difference in artistic achievement or imaginative expression. The relations in which a particular work stands can make an essential difference to the nature of the work – and thus to how it should be treated. For without recognising the importance of such relations we could not explain why certain attitudes towards works of originality, pastiches and fakes are appropriate (Kieran 2004).

I am not denying that much of what is important about artistic value concerns experience. How worthwhile is the experience a work affords? Does the experience give us pleasure, insight or understanding? These are questions importantly tied to the values of art. Indeed, in many cases a work's value may just be a function of the experiences provoked. But it is not true of all art. Sometimes we value our experience with original works because of the prior recognition that what has been achieved is a genuine artistic achievement. Leonardo's *Last Supper* or Picasso and Braque's cubism, just as Wittgenstein's *Tractatus* or Einstein's theory of relativity, would have been achievements whether or not anyone had ever gone on to experience, read or understand them. And it would have been a worse world had those things not been achieved.

## Conclusion

We often value original works because they are constitutive of the artistic achievement or imaginative expression of an artist. The values of art are not entirely reducible to the value of the experiences afforded. Hence art bears an interesting relation to the sacred. Unlike icons considered in terms of the sacred, art works are neither a divine intimation nor, at least where originals matter, substitutable. But they can be, in a humanistic sense, as close as one can get. For they manifest one of the finest achievements of the human psyche: the embodiment, expression and crystallisation of artistic achievements and attempts to make sense of the world. As such they embody great qualities of mind, which is why we can learn from them, why we often value art so highly and why the destruction of works can be a desecration. Such an attitude is neither hard-wired into us nor should we seek to do without it.

## References

Davies, D. (2003) *Art as Performance*, Oxford: Blackwell.
Kieran, M. (2004) *Revealing Art*, London: Routledge.
Wood, M. (2002) 'Beauty and Terror', *Royal Academy Magazine* 77: 38–43.

# 5   Is Life Sacred?

## Suzanne Uniacke

Many people, including many of no religious persuasion, have a strong sense that life is sacred. References to the sacredness of life – and of human life in particular – are frequently invoked in public discussion. Why? The most obvious answer is the bearing that the sacredness or sanctity of life is thought to have on the morality of terminating life. Indeed it is a range of practical concerns about terminating life that have provided the context for much contemporary philosophical discussion of the claim that life is sacred. Such concerns include abortion, euthanasia, warfare, capital punishment, and a cluster of environmental problems that raise issues of life and death.

I have two primary aims in this essay. The first is to address the link between the sanctity of life and the morality of terminating life, and to argue that although these two issues are closely connected they should not be equated. Some philosophers writing on practical ethics seem to assume that if killing is morally permissible in some circumstances, then life is not sacred. This is not so. To make the same point from the other direction: in accepting that life is sacred we are not thereby committed to the view that killing is never permissible. The second of my aims is to explore whether there is a plausible secular sense in which life might be regarded as sacred.

## What is meant by the Question 'Is Life Sacred?'?

Some people might ask whether we really need to explore the question 'Is Life Sacred?' at all. Isn't the sanctity of human life a central principle or doctrine of western medical ethics, for instance? And of course it is. But that fact doesn't get us very far. For even in the context of medical ethics, where a principle or doctrine of the sanctity of human life might be regarded by many as enshrined, so to speak, there can be deep disagreement about its interpretation – what it means and implies – both in theory and in practice.

More general disagreement arises over the claim that life is sacred, partly because people can and do mean different things by it. A theist who says that life is sacred will mean, at least in part, that life, and more precisely human life, is made in God's image and that our lives belong to God, and that killing contravenes God's law, while an atheist will not be saying anything about God at all. Similarly, the claim that life is sacred might mean that life has a particular, special kind of value that is appropriately referred to as sacred, or that it is morally wrong to terminate life, or both of those things.

The claim that life has a special value, and the claim that it is morally wrong to terminate life, are frequently combined, intertwined, even taken as equivalent, in pronouncements about the sacredness or sanctity of life. These two claims are closely related of course, since the value that life has will have a significant bearing on the reasons why, and the conditions under which, it can be wrong to terminate life. The philosopher John Kleinig notes that

> it is only on the assumption of a certain "valuing" of "life"
> that an enquiry into the conditions under which it may be
> terminated is necessitated, and any justification of those

> conditions will need to take into account what may be said
> on its behalf.
>
> (Kleinig 1991: xv).

If life has a special value that is appropriately characterised as sacred, then the termination of life is morally a very serious matter.

Nevertheless, despite the close relationship between them, the question of the special value of life, and the question of the morality of terminating life, are distinguishable. The distinction is perhaps best explained by reference to examples. Say a person believes, as many people purport to do, that all human life is immensely and equally valuable: that the death of a human being is the loss of something of immense value, and that no one individual human being's life is more valuable than the life of another. She also believes that it is morally permissible to terminate human life – to kill – in some circumstances. Are these two beliefs consistent? The answer is yes.

Consider the moral permissibility of killing another person in self-defence. Of course some people hold an absolutist position that it is always impermissible to kill another person even in self-defence, and in support of this view they sometimes urge that all human life is equally valuable. However, the prevailing view is that the use of lethal force in genuine self-defence against an unjust attacker is a paradigm of morally permissible killing. And this latter view, it seems to me, is entirely consistent with the belief that all human life is immensely and equally valuable. How is this so?

The moral permissibility of self-defence need not imply that an unjust attacker's life is not valuable, nor even that it is less valuable than the life of the person who is being attacked. This point is frequently obscured because instances of permissible self-defence typically involve a situation in which an innocent person who is under attack uses necessary and proportionate force against an unjust attacker who is responsible and morally culpable on account of his actions. Such instances can easily lead us to assume that the use of lethal force in self-defence is permissible because when it comes to a forced choice between lives (the attacker's life or the victim's), the life of a culpable unjust attacker is less valuable, less worthy or worthwhile, than the life of the innocent victim. But unjust attackers – that is, those who attack unoffending persons – are not always responsible and culpable on account of their actions. And in such cases we also believe that self-defence is morally permissible: we accept that an unoffending person under unjust attack may defend his life, by using lethal force if necessary, against someone who is in fact morally blameless. An unjust attacker might be morally blameless because she is, for example, hallucinating or deranged; or else she might be acting under a reasonable mistake of fact on the basis of which she falsely believes that she herself is being attacked and that she is defending herself.[1]

Another example illustrates, from the other direction, that the value of life and the morality of terminating life are distinguishable issues. Think of a person with a very debilitating terminal illness who is in constant pain and who longs for death as a merciful release from her unrelenting suffering. This person's life is no longer inherently valuable to her; it is no longer a life that she considers to be in itself worthwhile. Other people who know what her life has become make a similar judgement and they hope for her sake that her suffering will soon be over, that she won't continue to linger in this terrible state. It does not follow from this that it would be morally permissible to terminate this person's life especially if (but not only if) to do so would contravene her wishes. Someone can hope that death will come soon but, for various reasons, not want to kill herself or to be killed. Moral objections to compassionate killing of a person whose life has, from various perspectives, ceased to be inherently valuable can arise from other types of considerations. They can be grounded in respect for a person's autonomy and for her own beliefs; they can arise from concern for others, or from more general concern about the nature or the consequences of killing, and so on.

The two examples above are intended to illustrate that (as in the case of self-defence) there are reasons that can ground the permissibility of killing that are independent of the inherent value of the particular life that is terminated, and that (as in the case of the suffering terminally ill person) killing can be wrong independently of the inherent value of the life in question. It might be argued, however, that this distinction would effectively collapse were we to take a particular view about the value of life, namely that life has *sacred* value. The objection that I am anticipating would maintain that the view that life has sacred value logically entails that it is always morally impermissible to terminate life. I want to reject this purported entailment. Whatever type of value life has or is believed to have, it is a substantive question whether it is morally permissible to terminate life. If the *value* of life is sacred – whatever 'sacred value' might be taken to mean – then it is nevertheless appropriate to ask whether, and for what reasons, it might be permissible to terminate or extinguish (instances of) such value. Could we be justified in terminating or destroying something of sacred value? This is a substantive question, even if our view of the value that life has always leads us to answer no.

In this essay I shall approach the question 'Is Life Sacred?' by thinking about what 'sacred value' might most plausibly be taken to mean in this context. There is already an extensive philosophical literature that discusses the so-called principle of the sanctity of life in relation to the morality of killing. The issues that surround the purported sanctity of life in this sense are very important, but they are too complex to be taken up here in addition to the less frequently discussed question of whether life has sacred value. Nevertheless, towards the conclusion of the essay I shall make some comments about the nature and the scope of the sanctity of life principle and its relation to the idea of life as having sacred value.

## What is meant by 'Sacred'?

The word 'sacred' has a number of senses. The two central ones listed in the *Oxford English Dictionary* are: (1) 'consecrated or held especially acceptable *to* a deity, dedicated or reserved or appropriate *to* some person or purpose; made holy by religious association, hallowed'; and (2) 'safeguarded or required by religion or reverence or tradition, indefeasible, inviolable, sacrosanct' (emphasis in original). Obviously the word 'sacred' has strongly religious connotations. Even so, neither of these two central senses is exclusively religious. The first sense is perhaps more religiously focused than the second. Something that is sacred in the first sense is *holy*. Nevertheless, the first sense allows that something can be sacred in virtue of its being dedicated or reserved or appropriate to some person or purpose, principally religious but not necessarily so. Something is sacred in the second sense if it is safeguarded or required by religion, sacrosanct. But sacredness in this second sense can also be due to non-religious tradition. Something that is sacred in the second sense is *inviolable*.

Both of these central senses of 'sacred' admit of purely secular interpretation in particular contexts. I shall confine my discussion to this interpretation. This is not to deny that life might be sacred in a religious sense, although in fact I do not subscribe to those views. However, my aim here is to explore whether life might plausibly be said to be sacred on a secular interpretation of the first of the general senses of 'sacred' distinguished above. Within that context, it seems to me that the challenge posed by the question 'Is life sacred?', is whether there is a plausible secular near-analogue of 'holy' that is applicable to life.

The two dictionary senses of 'sacred' listed above more or less correspond to the distinction that I have been emphasising between the idea that life has a special value appropriately referred to as sacred, as opposed to the sense in which reference to the 'sanctity of life' makes a claim about the morality of terminating life. Something that is sacred in the first sense has special value such that it is appropriately *prized* or *revered* on some basis and thus deserves to be honoured or respected.

If life is sacred in the first sense of being appropriately prized or revered, then this value is *extinguished* by or *lost* upon *death*, howsoever death should come about. Something that is sacred in the second sense is *protected, inviolable*: it is immune from or secured against infringement, interference or attack. Sacredness in the second sense is *infringed* or *violated* by *killing*. Of itself, death does not infringe or violate sacredness in this second sense. Something might be, perhaps most often is, safeguarded, protected, inviolable on account of its being appropriately prized or revered; and the claim that life is sacred seems often to express this combination of the two views: that life has special value and, for this reason, terminating life is wrong. But, as I have argued, these two senses in which something might be said to be sacred are distinguishable.

## Does Life have Sacred Value?

Before we can address the question of whether life is sacred in the first sense – whether it is appropriately prized or revered – it is important to clarify what we take life to be. 'Life' admits of two contrasts: life contrasts with death; and the living, the animate, also contrasts with the non-living, the inanimate (Kleinig 1991: 29). The fact that a discussion of whether life is sacred is focused on one of these contrasts rather than the other is often, it seems to me, a significant factor in what life is taken to be.

## Life Contrasted with Death

The contrast of life with death, for instance, tends to lead to an inquiry about when the loss of life is not a bad thing. Usually this line of inquiry then leads to an examination of the conditions under which *our* death is not something to be regretted as the loss or extinction of something that we value. The underlying concern of inquiries of this type is very often whether life is sacred in the second sense. The context of these discussions is the question of the morality of terminating life, and of terminating human life in particular, in a range of practical contexts such as abortion, euthanasia and warfare. This concern with the sanctity or inviolability of life also contributes to an emphasis on the conditions under which what some writers refer to as our *biographical* lives have value. Our biographical lives are best explained as our lives *as lived* as opposed to our physical or biological lives. Our biographical lives are the lives that we *lead* as opposed to the physical or biological lives that we *have* (Rachels 1983; Kleinig 1991: 41; Dworkin 1995: 82). This approach to the question of the sanctity of life then takes judgements about the quality of an individual's *subjective* life – her life as experienced by her – as crucial to the value of her biographical life. (Ronald Dworkin distinguishes the subjective value a life has for the person whose life it is as its *personal* value (Dworkin 1995: 73, emphasis original).) There is a very prominent strand of philosophical discussion about the value of life that proceeds along these lines. It examines the conditions under which the loss of an individual's life is not a tragedy for that individual; it addresses the conditions under which we regard our lives as worth living and the conditions under which our lives cease to be so. In the context of this line of reasoning, it is frequently argued that at the extreme when a person loses all possibility of consciousness and thus of subjective experience, then her life is no longer intrinsically valuable. This is because there is no longer a subject leading the life in question: subjectively such a life is indistinguishable from death.

This reasoning about the value of life – as a life led by a *subject* – is strongly associated with ethical evaluation from a (broadly) utilitarian perspective, although it is not confined to that position. Those who approach the question of the value of life in this way argue that an individual's simply being alive in the biological sense has no intrinsic value; rather, an intrinsically valuable life requires at least that the form of life be conscious (Glover 1977; Singer 1993). As I think is the case more generally, this line of reasoning is partly due to a motivating interest in questions about the morality of terminating life in a range of practical contexts and in the conditions under which terminating life is permissible. But within utilitarian thinking this reasoning also has a more deeply theoretical explanation. The claim that it is only conscious life that can have intrinsic value arises directly from the general utilitarian theory of value. According to the version of utilitarianism known as classical utilitarianism, intrinsic value consists in the *experiences* of conscious, sentient beings. On this view, positive value consists in pleasure or happiness; negative value consists in pain or suffering. Those who subscribe to a distinguishable version of utilitarianism called preference utilitarianism assign positive intrinsic value to the fulfilment of preferences (desires) and negative intrinsic value to the contravention of preferences. Preference utilitarianism can arguably attribute positive or negative intrinsic value to the fulfilment or contravention of someone's preferences (desires) in the absence of a corresponding conscious experience on the part of the subject whose preferences they are. (Thus, for example, the fulfilment or contravention of my desire that I not be lied to about something could have intrinsic value even if I were never to know one way or the other.) Nonetheless, for preference utilitarianism the possession of preferences (desires) itself requires consciousness. A living being that is not conscious is incapable of having preferences in the relevant sense, and so is incapable of intrinsic value. Further, on this view positive and negative intrinsic value will *mostly* involve corresponding experiences on the part of the subjects whose preferences are either fulfilled or contravened (Singer 1993; Uniacke 2002).

According to a utilitarian theory of value, life as such has no intrinsic value and individual lives are not intrinsically valuable as lives. Rather, on this view conscious individuals are said to be valuable as the 'bearers' or 'receptacles' of their positive experiences (pleasure, happiness, or preference fulfilment). Any life will have positive value only in so far as it makes certain types of experiences possible. It follows from this view that individual lives, and also forms of life, that are incapable of positive experiences do not and cannot possess intrinsic value. Thus, the lives of non-conscious organisms can have only instrumental value and such lives are valuable only in so far as they contribute to the positive experiences of conscious, sentient beings such as ourselves. Two further implications of this position are, first, that *conscious* lives that are incapable of pleasure, happiness or preference fulfilment can have no positive intrinsic value. Second, conscious lives that contain positive experiences that are outweighed by negative ones (for example, lives with much suffering and few pleasures) are not positively intrinsically valuable all things considered. This latter implication of utilitarianism contrasts with the view expressed by Thomas Nagel, that it is true of such lives that the experience itself can be significant irrespective of its contents.

> There are elements which, if added to one's experience, make life better; there are other elements which, if added to one's experience, make life worse. But what remains when these are set aside is not merely *neutral*: it is emphatically positive. Therefore life is worth living even when the bad elements of experience are plentiful, and the good ones too meager to outweigh the bad ones on their own. The additional positive weight is supplied by experience itself, rather than by any of its contents.
>
> (Nagel 1979: 2).

Further, a person can value being alive, and desperately want to go on living simply as an experiencing subject, despite the dreadfulness of all or most of her experiences. And to value being alive as an experiencing subject, as opposed to non-existence (death), is not irrational or unreasonable.

Of course the basic utilitarian view that intrinsic value can only subsist in sentient, conscious life is not universally accepted. For instance, many people believe that embryonic and early fetal human life has intrinsic value even though such life is not (yet) conscious or sentient. Further, a view that is strongly associated with deep ecology maintains that the phenomenon of life itself, individual biological lives, and also species-life and the integrated 'life' of eco-systems, all have intrinsic value. This essay is not the place to attempt a comprehensive argument about which living things might plausibly be said to have intrinsic value and why. However, it seems to me that a focus on the value of conscious life, and on the moral implications of the permanent loss of consciousness, is more appropriate to an inquiry about the morality of terminating life than it is to the more general question of whether life is sacred in the first sense. The view that we take about the morality of terminating (human) life may well be closely related to the possession and continuation of those features that, for the most part, give positive value to our subjective or personal lives. Nevertheless, physical or biological life – the fact that something is a living organism – might be appropriately prized or revered for other reasons.

## Life Contrasted with Non-Life

The question of the intrinsic value of physical or biological life – of the 'livingness of an organism ... as the site of self-integrating and self-renewing metabolic processes' (Kleinig 1991: 31) – tends to arise from a different contrast than that between life and death. Typically it arises from the contrast between life and non-life – the animate as distinct from the inanimate – and it focuses on biological life as emerging and evolving from the inanimate and as being valuable in itself as an 'awe-inspiring' achievement of natural processes. In this context, biological life might be regarded as a kind of primary material good (Kohl 2001). John Kleinig argues more fully along these lines, that

> there is manifest in living organisms a distinctive *independ-*
> *ence* of their environment that may evoke our affirmation
> and regard. By virtue of their self-integrating and self-
> renewing character, living organisms actively maintain their
> identity in a world that is constantly impinging upon them.
> Unlike inert substances, which passively retain an identity
> over time, and unlike inorganic matter, which offers no

> resistance to the impersonal forces of nature, the ability of a
> living organism to maintain its being – both individually and
> reproductively – in a dynamic interaction with its environ-
> ment may be seen as an achievement, an accomplishment,
> something that we can marvel at and esteem.
>
> (Kleinig 1991: 171, emphasis in original)

This reasoning captures, it seems to me, the essence of what people mean when they claim that life itself – both the phenomenon of life and the fact that a thing is physically alive – has intrinsic value independently of the form of life it is or of the quality of life it has.

The most prominent recent account of the sacredness of biological human life, in the sense of its being something to be prized or revered, is that of Ronald Dworkin in *Life's Dominion*. I should note that Dworkin's discussion might be taken to be an exception to my own contention above, that an underlying concern about the morality of terminating human life tends to lead to a more narrowly focused inquiry about the value of a subjective or personal life – of a life worth living – as distinct from a discussion of the special value of life as opposed to non-life. This is because Dworkin's discussion of the sacredness of biological life in *Life's Dominion* arises in the context of a broader argument about the termination of life, specifically as applied to abortion and euthanasia. In fact, Dworkin's emphasis on the sacredness of life in the first sense is due to his particular analysis of the nature of the moral disagreement about abortion and euthanasia. Dworkin argues that the source of (much of the) moral disagreement about the termination of life in these two contexts is due to the fact that a normal, successful human life represents, he claims, two types of creative investment – natural and human – both of which contribute to its value. According to Dworkin, *all* life represents or embodies natural investment as the product of evolutionary creation. Thus, all death is a waste or loss of the value that a living being has *because of what it embodies or represents. Human* lives also represent and embody the *creative human investment* of the subject of the life and of others. Dworkin then argues that much disagreement about the morality of abortion is best understood in terms of these dual investments: such disagreement reflects 'deep differences about the relative moral importance of the natural and human contributions to the inviolability of individual human lives'. Conservatives and liberals who disagree about the morality of abortion or of euthanasia do so according to Dworkin, 'not because one side wholly rejects a value [natural or human] that the other thinks cardinal, but because they take different – sometimes dramatically different – positions about the relative importance of these values, which both recognise as fundamental and profound' (Dworkin 1995: 91–92).

An assessment of Dworkin's diagnosis of the nature of moral disagreement about abortion and euthanasia is well beyond the scope of this essay. However, what Dworkin has to say about the value of all biological life as embodying or representing a natural investment is of direct relevance to my focus on the sacredness of life in the first sense. Here there are three fundamental aspects of Dworkin's account that are worthy of critical attention. The first is Dworkin's tendency to equivocate between the notions of sacredness and of intrinsic value; the second aspect is his equation of sacredness and inviolability; and the third and perhaps most important aspect is what Dworkin takes intrinsic value to be. I shall now discuss these three issues in turn.

## The Sacred and Intrinsic Value

As to Dworkin's tendency to equivocate between sacred and intrinsic value, it might seem uncontroversial to say that something that is appropriately regarded as sacred has intrinsic value, in the sense that it is prized for its own sake as distinct from being valued instrumentally as serving some end or aim. But if we look to the definition of 'sacred' that I quoted earlier, we see that something can be sacred *by association.* The notion of sacredness by association allows the possibility that the non-instrumental value of a sacred thing might not be due to its *inherent* features. Something that has no inherently valuable features might be valued for its own sake – non-instrumentally – by virtue of its association. In a religious context, a piece of cloth believed to be part of Christ's garment might be prized and revered not for its inherent features (for example, its quality, colour or texture) but as, and only as, part of Christ's garment. A site might be regarded as sacred because, and only because, it was the site of an apparition. Non-religiously, objects that acquire the status of national symbols, such as national flags, might be revered not as objects in themselves (e.g. as pieces of cloth with particular colours and patterns) but because, and only because, of what they have come to represent. If the description of something as having *intrinsic value* typically implies that it possesses *inherent* value – that its value derives from its inherent features – then in cases of sacredness by association it would seem better to speak of the (sacred) thing simply as being non-instrumentally valuable, as distinct from its being intrinsically valuable.

There is a second, more important point to be made about Dworkin's tendency to equivocate between sacred and intrinsic value, and that is that irrespective of whether all sacred things possess intrinsic (inherent) value it is not at all obvious that anything that has intrinsic value is appropriately regarded as sacred. Consider happiness, for instance. Many, probably most, people regard happiness (however they might conceive of it) as intrinsically valuable, as being valuable for its own sake, because of its inherent features or what it is. But happiness is not *sacred*; indeed it would seem very odd (not simply mistaken) to characterise it as such. Something that is sacred is not simply prized for its own sake, as happiness is. Rather, the sacred is appropriately *honoured* or *revered*.

The honour or reverence that is due to a sacred thing arises from the source or nature of its intrinsic or non-instrumental value. What is sacred in the religious sense is not simply intrinsically or non-instrumentally valuable, but *holy*. And the same distinction must apply to a secular sense of 'sacred'. For the term 'sacred' to be applicable in a secular sense we must invoke conditions in addition to, and over and above, the concept of intrinsic or non-instrumental value. Secular 'sacred value' requires a secular analogue of holiness. Thus, it is no accident that in characterizing life as sacred Dworkin and other writers refer to life as being 'marvellous in itself', 'awe-inspiring', and so on. Something that is sacred is a worthy object of certain types of profound response on our part, such as marvel, awe, respect or reverence. To be fair, Dworkin does not simply equate sacredness with intrinsic value. (Nevertheless, in distinguishing two categories of intrinsically valuable things – the incrementally valuable and the inviolable – he does say that the latter are sacred (Dworkin 1995: 70).) However, his discussion is not sufficiently forthcoming about the difference between those features of biological life in virtue of which such life might appropriately be regarded as being *sacred*, as distinct from its having 'merely' intrinsic value.

## Sacredness and Inviolability

The second aspect of Dworkin's account of the sacred that I want to address is his explicit equation of sacredness and inviolability: Dworkin uses these terms interchangeably. As my earlier discussion of the two central senses of 'sacred' implies, this equation of sacredness (sacred value) and inviolability suppresses a significant distinction. The sacred value of a thing arises from what it is, from what it embodies or from what it represents. Something that has sacred value *ought* to be honoured and protected for what it is or for what it represents. Dworkin seems to express this particular distinction by saying that something is inviolable when its deliberate destruction would dishonour what ought to be honoured (Dworkin 1995: 73–74). Thus, the sacred ought not to be violated or attacked *because of* the (sacred) value that it embodies or represents. The mistake that can arise here is to think that the notions of sacredness and inviolability are equivalent. They are, on the contrary, distinguishable notions. 'Sacred' refers to a value that is possessed by things that appropriately inspire awe, marvel, reverence or respect. 'Inviolability' refers to the way in which a sacred thing ought to be treated: it ought not to be violated or attacked.

## Varieties of Intrinsic Value

Third, there can be deep disagreement about the basis on which something has intrinsic value. Disagreement arises about whether intrinsic value is inherent or is, in some sense, bestowed. Is something intrinsically valuable because we value it for its own sake? Or is its intrinsic value inherent in the sense that it is independent of anyone's valuing it, even independent of the possibility of its being valued? Could something be intrinsically valuable even if there were to be no one, and could be no one, to value it? Kleinig argues that all value requires that there be a valuer, that is, someone or something who values. If we accept this, as I shall do for the sake of argument, it doesn't follow that intrinsic value is merely subjective. If something's having intrinsic value depends on there being a valuer, intrinsic value is not thereby simply a matter of what that valuer *happens* to value for its own sake (non-instrumentally). As valuers we value things intrinsically. But we could be wrong in so valuing something that is not worthy of being valued for its own sake, as what it is or represents. Conversely, we might not value something intrinsically which we ought so to value. We might be ignorant or fail to recognise the features of something in virtue of which it is valuable for its own sake (Kleinig 1991: 8–10).

There is a significant distinction between the view that something is intrinsically valuable when it is (objectively) *valuable for its own sake*, as opposed to the view that something is intrinsically valuable *if we value it intrinsically*, for its own sake. The latter view is consistent with the belief that intrinsic value is entirely subjective; on this view, intrinsic value might simply be a matter of what we happen to value for its own sake. Dworkin's discussion of the intrinsic value of life, it seems to me, comes down on the side of the latter view. While he says that intrinsic value is independent of our needs, this is simply to say that intrinsic value is not instrumental value in the obvious sense. (When we value something intrinsically we value it for its own sake and not because it serves some end or aim.) But Dworkin also maintains that we are *selective* about *what we value intrinsically* (Dworkin 1995: 80). He notes that there are degrees of the sacred (not everything that has sacred value for us has equal value), and that our convictions about the inviolability of the sacred are selective: they are, he says, shaped by and reflect our *needs and opinions*. This claim implies, it seems to me, that for Dworkin the basis of our selectivity about what we value for its own sake is deeply instrumental.

Dworkin does not himself buy into the issue of whether life is intrinsically valuable or sacred. He says that it is not his purpose to defend the positions that he explains (Dworkin 1995: 81). Rather, his concern is to identify the bases on which we hold that life is sacred. He does so against a more general account of how something *becomes sacred for us*. According to Dworkin, something becomes sacred for a given culture or person; thus it is sacred by association or designation – sacred through its history (Dworkin 1995: 78). The 'nerve of the sacred' lies in the value *we attach* to a process or enterprise or project rather than to its results considered independently of how they were produced (Dworkin 1995: 81). Dworkin speaks of the sacred as having normative significance *for us*. This is consistent with a deeply subjectivist view of intrinsic value: what is intrinsically valuable is what we value for its own sake. Whether we appropriately so value something, and whether this is a legitimate question, are issues on which Dworkin's account is silent.

Dworkin also maintains that in valuing life intrinsically, we value life on the basis of the *processes that produce it*. But surely a process that produces something as its outcome is not an inherent feature of that outcome. Thus, on Dworkin's view, while we value life for its own sake (non-instrumentally), this valuing of life is not based on life's *inherent* features. Dworkin compares our valuing of life with the way in which (he says) we value art. He maintains that loss of the value of life is intrinsically bad – 'objectively a shame' (whatever that means) – in the same way that destruction of great art or the loss of important knowledge would be. But do we value art in the way that Dworkin says we do? Do we value art, irrespective of its artistic quality, on the basis of the creative processes that produce it? Surely we judge the *intrinsic* value of art on the basis of the *product* as well. We value art selectively, and in so doing we appeal to its *inherent* features.

Kleinig's account of the intrinsic value of life provides an important contrast to the account offered by Dworkin. Kleinig does locate the purported intrinsic value of biological life in its *inherent* features: its self-integrating and self-renewing character, its dynamic interaction with its environment. He maintains that these features may in themselves be seen as an achievement, an accomplishment, something that we can marvel at and esteem. In response to Dworkin's view that we value life on the basis of the processes that produce it, we can ask whether it is relevant to the intrinsic value of life's *inherent* features how they were produced. What if something with a self-integrating and self-renewing character and a dynamic interaction with its environment were to be produced some other way (not creatively by God or by evolution), or what if we were simply ignorant of how life is produced? Could we still marvel at the phenomenon of life all the same? It seems to me that the answer is yes. Consider also the long-standing and widespread fascination we have with whether life exists elsewhere in the universe. This fascination might be construed as a search for extraterrestrial intelligence, as opposed to an interest in whether there is any biological life beyond Earth. But this is, I think, mistaken. The predictable response to evidence of the existence of *any* life elsewhere in the universe would be that of wild excitement. Why? It seems to me that the answer is that the very existence of life, with its inherent features, strikes us as 'near-miraculous'. As Paul Davies has put it, 'Life is a weird and exceedingly special state of matter' (Davies 2003). That life with its inherent features can emerge from non-animate matter is awe-inspiring, something about which we marvel.

## Conclusion

If life is sacred in the first sense – something to be prized for its inherent features and about which it is appropriate to marvel – then something highly valuable is extinguished or lost when a living thing dies, however it dies. As to the morality of the termination of life, I have emphasised that this is a distinguishable issue. If life has sacred value, this can imply that once it exists life ought to be protected and preserved, and that we can fail to accord life its due respect by violating it in various ways, for example in attacking it directly. The fact that life has sacred value does not imply, however, that life must be preserved or protected independently of other considerations or at all costs.

## Note

1  The moral consideration that grounds the permissibility of the use of force in self-defence against an unjust attack, irrespective of the attacker's culpability or blamelessness, is that self-defensive force directly wards off the infliction of an otherwise irreparable injustice. This is something that, within moral limits, as unoffending persons we have a positive right to do. It does not follow from this, however, that killing in self-defence is always morally justified all things considered, irrespective of the comparative number or value of the lives involved. I have argued for this view in detail elsewhere (Uniacke 1994).

## References

Davies, P. (2003), 'Is Anyone out There?', *The Guardian*, 22 January.

Dworkin, R. (1995) *Life's Dominion*, London: Harper Collins.

Glover, J. (1977) *Causing Death and Saving Lives*, Harmondsworth: Penguin.

Kleinig, J. (1991) *Valuing Life*, New Jersey: Princeton University Press.

Kohl, M. (1974) *The Morality of Killing*, New Jersey: Humanities Press.

Kohl, M. (2001), 'Life and Death', in Laurence Becker and Charlotte Becker (eds) *Encyclopedia of Ethics*, New York: Routledge.

McMahan, J. (2002) *The Ethics of Killing*, Oxford: Oxford University Press.

Nagel, T. (1979) 'Death', in Nagel, *Mortal Questions*, Cambridge: Cambridge University Press.

Rachels, J. (1986) *The End of Life: Euthanasia and Morality*, Oxford: Oxford University Press.

Singer, P. (1993) *Practical Ethics*, 2nd edn, Cambridge: Cambridge University Press.

Uniacke, S. (1994) *Permissible Killing: The Self-defence Justification of Homicide*, Cambridge: Cambridge University Press.

Uniacke, S. (2002) 'A Critique of the Preference Utilitarian Argument Against Killing People', *Australasian Journal of Philosophy*, 80: 209–217.

# 6 The Sacred and the Profane

## Simona Giordano and John Harris

In 'Is Life Sacred?' Suzanne Uniacke discusses the relation between the value of life and the morality of terminating life. She notices that pronouncements about the sacredness of life and pronouncements about the wrongness of terminating life often go together. She writes:

> The claim that *life has a special value*, and the claim that it is morally wrong *to terminate life*, are frequently combined, intertwined, even taken as equivalent, in pronouncements about the sacredness or sanctity of life. These two claims are closely related of course, since *the value that life has* will have a significant bearing on the reasons why, and the conditions under which, it can be wrong *to terminate life* . . . . If *life has a special value* that is appropriately characterised as sacred, then the *termination of life* is morally a very serious matter.
>
> (pp. 60–61 this volume, our emphasis)

On the one hand, those who believe that life is sacred also believe that terminating life is wrong; on the other, those who believe that life is not sacred, also think that terminating life may be permissible. The latter, Uniacke points out, often appeal to the fact that terminating life is sometimes accepted (such as in self-defence) to demonstrate that life is not sacred.

Uniacke objects to both groups of contenders that the value of life and the morality of killing are two 'distinguishable' issues (p. 61 and p. 79), and that the morality of killing is not necessarily related to the value of life.

The separation between these two issues has two major implications:

1  Even if in some particular instances terminating life may be permissible, this is no evidence that life is not valuable in itself (or inherently valuable, or intrinsically valuable – Uniacke uses all these terms to denote the value of life, and we shall see later their meaning in her work).
2  Even if in some particular instances life is not (or no longer) *inherently or intrinsically valuable*, terminating life may still be wrong.

The meaning of this last statement is not that it may be wrong to destroy something that is not intrinsically valuable because this something may be *extrinsically* valuable, that is, valuable to someone else or for some reason other than the fact that *it is*. Some people may argue for example that an embryo is not intrinsically valuable, but it may still be wrong to destroy it if its life is important to other people. When Uniacke argues that it may be wrong to kill a life that is not intrinsically valuable she is not proposing this argument. She seems to be objecting to the permissibility of acts of euthanasia.

The second implication, thus, has great ethical relevance, as it seems to entail a claim against people's entitlement to make at least some end-of-life decisions.

Uniacke illustrates her point of view about people's entitlement to make decisions to end their own life with the following example:

> Think of a person with a very debilitating terminal illness,
> who is in constant pain and who longs for death as a merci-
> ful release from her unrelenting suffering. This person's
> life is no longer inherently valuable to her; it is no longer a
> life that she considers to be in itself worthwhile. Other
> people who know what her life has become make a similar
> judgement and they hope for her sake that her suffering
> will soon be over, that she won't continue to linger in this
> terrible state. It does not follow from this that it would be
> morally permissible to terminate this person's life
> especially if (*but not only if*) to do so would contravene her
> wishes.
>
> (p. 62; our emphasis)

Thus, according to Uniacke, it is impermissible to terminate a person's life, 'not only if to do so would contravene her wishes' but also, as we understand it, if this *does not* contravene her wishes. It seems to follow from this that, according to Uniacke, even if a person in such a terrible state asked to have her pains terminated, complying with her wishes may still be wrong.

In the following sections, we shall discuss Uniacke's arguments. Our conclusions will only partly differ from Uniacke's, but this differ-ence is crucial and has important ethical consequences, especially in terms of people's entitlement to decide whether to continue to live or not.

We may briefly anticipate our disagreement and conclusions as follows:

For Uniacke, if killing may be permissible, it is *not* because life is not sacred.

We shall demonstrate that if killing is not permissible, it is not because life is sacred.

## 'LIFE' and 'THE VALUE OF LIFE'

Uniacke's views about the sacredness of life and the permissibility of killing follow from her understanding of life and the value of life. When Uniacke discusses 'life', she tends to utilise the notion in an impersonal way. She discusses the 'sacredness or sanctity of life', the morality of 'terminating life', 'the value that life has', and so on (rather than the value of people's lives, or the morality of killing people). 'Life', in Uniacke's work, is represented as a subject in itself, which has value in itself (inherent, intrinsic value), and which is substantially independent of persons or living beings. Persons, and other living beings, are for Uniacke 'instances of such value' (life) (p. 63). From now on we shall therefore use 'LIFE' and 'VALUE OF LIFE' (capitalised) to refer to Uniacke's notions of LIFE and VALUE, as separated from individual lives; and we shall use 'life' and 'value of life' (lower case) to refer to individuals' living (being alive) and to the value that living individuals attach to their living (to their life).

If Uniacke is right, and LIFE is a VALUE of which I am only an instance, what importance might the value that *I* attach to my life have? For Uniacke, not surprisingly, not much. Uniacke in fact argues that the VALUE OF LIFE is independent of the value that I may attach to my life. 'Value', Uniacke writes, 'is not simply a matter of what the valuer happens to value' (p. 76). Uniacke's theory appears as a typical example of philosophical dualism: there seem to be two planes, one of LIFE *in itself*, and the other of the living creatures, 'instances of such value' (p. 63). The VALUE OF LIFE is not 'merely subjective' (p. 76), and is independent of the value that an individual 'may believe' their life to have.

Uniacke's arguments raise important questions. How should we understand LIFE? As a separate substance, a 'breath' that animates creatures? Or rather as a 'concept' of mind? What is LIFE abstractly meant, as unrelated to living beings? And what do we mean when we say that LIFE – in its abstract form – has value?

Uniacke herself poses the question of 'what we take life to be' (p. 66), but she does not provide an answer. However, we may notice that, every time she gives an example of what she means by 'LIFE' and the 'VALUE OF LIFE', she has to refer to *living creatures.* For example, while discussing the morality of terminating LIFE, she gives the example of self-defence and the example of the person with a terminal illness who wishes to have her pains ended; in both examples terminating LIFE consists in killing a person (pp. 61–63). When, later on in her essay, Uniacke talks about the VALUE OF LIFE, she refers to 'individual biological lives, and also species-life and . . . eco-systems' (p. 69).

Thus, on the one hand, for Uniacke LIFE is a subject in itself, maybe a 'substance' separated from living individuals, which has VALUE in itself (inherent and intrinsic), that is, which has VALUE independently of the value that individuals 'happen to' attach to their lives (p. 76). On the other hand, however, every time she attempts to clarify what she means by LIFE and by the VALUE OF LIFE, she needs to talk of situations in which persons may find themselves. This illustrates the conceptual difficulty we meet when we try to think about LIFE as something above and beyond living beings.

## What we should 'take life to be'

As we continuously experience and observe living beings, ranging from human beings to any other member of the animals as well as of the vegetable realm, it may seem to us that there is something such as LIFE, a 'breath' that enlivens them, some sort of thing that these beings possess when they are alive, and that maybe they cease to possess when they are no longer alive. Thus, we often use expressions such as 'this person had a very good life', 'there is a lot life can offer', or similar. However, it seems to us that we use these expressions in a somewhat metaphorical sense. What we actually mean, when we say that 'this person had a very good life', is that 'she enjoyed "being in the world", and that she had a lot of things to be happy about', and not that 'life' was something she actually possessed and which was of a good quality – as we would say of her car 'she had a very good car'.

LIFE should be understood as an idea that we frame, by means of abstraction, from the observation of living beings. We experience and observe living beings, and may infer that there is LIFE. But, of course, the fact that there are living beings does not mean that there is a LIFE 'separated' from them, and our eventual deduction that something such as LIFE actually exists may say something about the way our minds work, about our psychology, but seems to say nothing about how things in fact are.[1]

When we ask the question of, as Uniacke puts it, 'what we take life to be' (p. 66), we seem compelled to admit that LIFE can only be understood in terms of beings that are alive. All our considerations about life include reference to living beings. Saying that 'life is beautiful' means no more than saying that living may be a very positive experience for someone, or that a person values and enjoys observing other living beings; saying that 'life is sad' means nothing more than that sometimes living beings suffer; and, as we have pointed out above, when we say that 'there may be life' on other planets all we mean is that there may be living creatures there.

If all we mean, when we say that for example 'life is beautiful', is that sometimes living beings are happy to live and have positive experiences, and if all we mean when we say that 'life is sad' is that sometimes living beings are not happy and have negative experiences, then also when we state that 'life is valuable' all we mean is that normally living beings enjoy and value living. And the statement that 'life is *inherently* valuable', that it is 'valuable in itself', as opposed to 'instrumentally valuable', if it means anything, can only mean that sometimes living beings prefer to live and would carry on living independently of the conditions in which they are living. We should conclude that statements such as 'life is sacred' or 'is valuable' or similar must necessarily refer to the value that individuals attach to living, to how they consider or feel about living.

## The Ethics of Killing and Preserving Lives

The VALUE OF LIFE can only be understood in terms of the value of individual living beings, and, more particularly, of the value they attach to their own life (to the fact that they are alive and to the conditions in which they live). Thus it is not LIFE that has value or can be regarded as sacred or sacrosanct or intrinsically valuable; but rather it is living creatures that are valuable – not because they are *alive* (they have 'LIFE') but because *they* are alive, and are creatures who matter. (They value living, and, generally, living in certain conditions, and/or they are valuable to others.)

This has important implications with regard to the ethics of killing and preserving lives. It is from the point of view of the value of *persons* that we should analyse the ethics of killing and preserving lives, and not from the point of view of the VALUE OF LIFE in itself. Therefore the 'morality of terminating life' (p. 61) should be properly understood as the morality of killing. As we shall shortly see, we agree with Uniacke that killing may be permissible in some circumstances, not simply because the ethics of terminating life and the value of life are two 'distinguishable issues', but because the VALUE OF LIFE is nothing more than the value that people attach to living. When analysing the morality of killing, we need to distinguish three cases, the *value of life* being different in each:

1  Killing a person who values life and wishes to live.
2  Killing a creature that cannot be considered as a person.
3  Killing a person who no longer values life and wishes to die.

**Killing a person who values life and wishes to live** is *prima facie* wrong (although, as Uniacke points out, there may be circumstances in which it may be acceptable, such as in self-defence), but the nature of this wrong requires further analysis. According to Uniacke, if killing is permissible, this is not because LIFE is not sacred. We object to this that if killing is ever not permissible or wrong it is not because LIFE is sacred. LIFE, in fact cannot be sacred or not sacred. The nature of the wrong done when an individual who wishes to live is killed does not lie in the violation of the VALUE OF LIFE, but lies instead in the violation of the individual's preference to continue to live. If killing is wrong, it is because the individual who lives has value, and the fact she values living is what gives value to her life. We understand by 'persons' any individuals who have this capacity to value living. Many characterisations of 'personhood' have been attempted in philosophy, but at the basis of all these characterisations there is, we believe, a fundamental concept: a person is a creature who is able to value his or her being alive. Thus understood, persons might, in principle, be members of any species, or even machines, capable of valuing existence.[2] Valuing LIFE in terms of the person who values living yields an explanation of the wrong done to individuals when they are killed against their wishes. On this account, to kill, or to fail to sustain the life of a person, is to deprive that individual of something they value, and the wrong consists in this deprivation – in the frustration of the individual's wish to live.

**Killing a creature that cannot be considered as a person** cannot, on this account, represent a wrong to that creature. Non-persons or potential persons cannot be wronged by being destroyed, not because they 'do not possess' or 'are not instances of' LIFE but rather because they cannot enjoy or value living and therefore cannot be wronged by its loss. If they are deprived of life they do not thereby lose anything that they can value or wish not to lose. Since the value of LIFE is neither more nor less than the value of those who value their living, destroying a creature which is and can only be indifferent to living cannot figure as a violation of the value of that creature's life.

This does not mean that our acts towards creatures that do not have a personal life can *never* be wrong. The account we have given of the idea of 'LIFE' and of the importance of 'persons' does not of course exhaust the wrongs that might be done in ending or failing to sustain the 'life' or existence of sentient creatures. Some of these wrongs will have to do with causing pain or suffering. Some others will have to do with wrongs that may be done to those persons who take a benevolent interest in the individual concerned. However, our account shows that killing a creature that does not have a personal life cannot be wrong in the same sense or in the same way in which it is wrong to kill a person who wishes to live.[3] The value of life is to be understood as the value that an individual attaches to living, and consequently, in cases in which the subject cannot value living, the moral relevance of acts towards that creature is profoundly different from the moral relevance of acts towards creatures which have and enjoy a personal life – living.

**Killing a person who no longer values life and wishes to die** may be permissible, or even right, for the same reason for which killing someone who wishes to live is generally wrong. If killing in these cases is permissible, or right, it is not because LIFE is not sacred (as LIFE is neither sacred nor not sacred). Killing a person, or helping her to die, may be permissible and indeed right because the individual who lives has value, and the value of her life is the value she believes her being 'in the world' to have. Respect for 'LIFE' cannot logically and therefore ethically be disjoined from respect for the individual who lives. Thus, if, on the one hand, persons who want to live are wronged by being killed because they are thereby deprived of something they value, on the other hand, persons who do not wish to continue to live are not on this account harmed by having their wish to die granted, through voluntary euthanasia, for example. Death, any death, as we have remarked above, cannot logically be a violation of LIFE, as LIFE is not separable from individuals' living. It can only be a violation of a person, and of her preference to continue to live. If what matters is the person's evaluation and wishes relating to whether or not living is desirable or good for them, the same wrong that is done to an individual when they are killed against their wishes is done when they are kept alive against their wishes. The wrong has the *same* moral nature and weight. It is, in both cases, a violation of the person and of her choices. It is, in both cases, a violation of the value of *persons*.[4]

## Conclusions

In this essay, we have analysed Uniacke's arguments relating to the value of life and permissibility of terminating life – of killing.

Uniacke, like many contemporary philosophers, has remained attached to a (we may say) Platonic concept of LIFE as a separate substance from individual lives. They believe they can sensibly talk about LIFE and its VALUE, and sensibly consider individuals as mere 'instances of such value'. We have objected, against this position, that there is no empirical or logical ground for asserting the existence of LIFE as something detached or detachable from living beings. If LIFE can only be understood in terms of individual lives, also the VALUE OF LIFE can only be understood if it is referred to the value of individual lives, and more particularly to the value they attach to their living.

This has important ethical implications, especially in terms of respect for people's decisions not to live. Denying the meaningfulness of the concept of LIFE, unless it is referred to living beings, and claiming that there is no VALUE beyond the value of living beings, and beyond the value they attach to being alive, is to admit that what counts morally are *persons* and all creatures that may be considered as such. Other things and other beings may count morally as well, but if they do count morally, they do so in ways beyond the scope of our present discussion. This means that *persons* are the pivot of the moral universe, that morality of acts is always to be related to the idea of respect for these special creatures. The value of life is violated every time a person's evaluation of his or her own life is disregarded. Every time a person's wish to continue to live, or not to continue to live, is violated, the value of life is also violated.

Life is not 'sacred' nor yet is it profane. What may be sacred, in some sense, are lives of a particular sort – the lives of persons. If it makes any sense to talk of the sacredness of human life, this must be (and can only be) understood in terms of respect for persons.

## Notes

1 The structure of this argument is drawn from David Hume's argument on causation. See D. Hume, *Treatise of Human Nature*, Oxford: Oxford University Press, 1967.

2 Machines with the capacities relevant to personhood might not of course be 'alive'. For this reason it might be preferable to speak of 'existence' rather than 'life'.

3 Of course some of the things that may be part of the wrong of killing, causing pain for example, may be common to both.

4 See for example John Harris, *The Value of Life*, London: Routledge, 1985, and Ronald Dworkin, *Life's Dominion.*

# 7    Is Liberty Sacred?

## Alan Haworth

My subject is liberalism, so I had better open by stating exactly what I take 'liberalism' to be. I shall then say why I think humanists – and, indeed, anyone likely to be reading this – should take more than a passing interest in liberalism (as I am about to define it). The greater part of this essay will be devoted to a problem to which I would like to find some sort of answer. I will set it out in detail when I come to it.

## What is Liberalism?

To begin with, then, liberals of the sort in which I am interested hold,

(i)     that each individual has certain rights (or 'liberties') which other individuals, and the state, are morally bound to respect;

(ii)    that these rights crucially include liberty of conscience (that is, the liberty to practise the religion of one's choice, or none), freedom of speech and expression, the freedom to live your life in your own way, and the freedom to lend or withdraw your consent from the government;

(iii)   that no society in which these rights are not – generally and on the whole – respected can be counted as a 'free society';

(iv)    (underpinning the above) that individual freedom – construed as autonomy or 'sovereignty' (J.S. Mill's word) – is of huge, if not supreme, importance.

In the sense of 'liberalism' at issue these tenets form the core of the liberal value-system. (I don't know whether it is right to describe liberals as holding liberty 'sacred', but it should be clear that they rank it very highly.) The writings of the great liberal philosophers – Locke's *Second Treatise of Civil Government* (Locke 1988), Mill's *On Liberty* (Mill 1991) and, more recently John Rawls's *A Theory of Justice* (Rawls 1972), to take three canonical examples – is devoted to their interpretation and defence. The tenets are, of course, differently expressed by different writers. But there are clear family resemblances between – for example – Locke's argument that we are the bearers of natural rights to life and liberty, Mill's insistence that there is a 'sphere of action in which society, as distinguished from the individual, has, if any, only an indirect interest' (1991: 16), and Rawls's that a 'just' society is structured, in part, by a specific range of 'basic liberties' available for every citizen to exercise (1972: 60ff).

The foregoing definition of 'liberalism' merits a number of observations. The first is that 'liberalism' and 'liberal' are words which can be used in a number of ways and which tend to be bandied about rather loosely. For example, 'liberal' is sometimes used by right-wingers, especially in North America, as a pejorative term for anyone who stands politically to the left of themselves (i.e. for pretty well everybody else). Certainly, Locke, Mill, and Rawls are liberals in this sense too, although it is not a sense of 'liberal' which captures the particular nature of their philosophical position. Again, 'liberalism' is sometimes used to refer to 'economic liberalism', that is, the doctrine of *laissez faire*. That is a perfectly legitimate sense of 'liberalism' but, by contrast, the liberalism at issue here has no especial connection with *laissez faire*. (As it happens, John Stuart Mill was both an economic liberal and a political liberal. In his view, there were good utilitarian reasons for both positions. However, in the absence of the utilitarian reasons, he could, quite logically, have abandoned the former view, and retained the latter.) Finally, something which, perhaps, ought to go without saying: There is no special relationship between the liberalism in which I am interested here and 'party political liberalism'; that is, the doctrine which happens to be embraced by the British, or any other, Liberal party at any particular time.

My second observation is that liberalism in the sense of 'liberalism' at issue – or plain 'liberalism' as I shall call it from here on – is compatible with a range of other beliefs. Belief in God and atheism are both compatible with liberalism. You can be a staunch advocate of economic *laissez faire*, or you can be a socialist, but you can be a liberal either way. Whether you are the former or the latter will depend on what *else* you believe. You may believe that it is only where the free market prevails that liberal institutions can flourish. Alternatively, you may believe that it is only with the triumph of socialism that such institutions, and the attitudes required to operate them successfully, can be fully realised. (Of course, you cannot consistently hold both beliefs, but it would be irrelevant to consider their relative merits here.)

Not that the range of possibilities is infinitely malleable. You can't be a liberal and a fascist, nor can you be a liberal and the sort of Marxist who adheres to a particular interpretation of Marx's claims that 'bourgeois notions of freedom, culture, law, etc.' are 'but the outgrowth of the conditions of your bourgeois production and bourgeois property' (Marx and Engels 1991: 48), that is, if you think liberalism is just so much 'ideology', and therefore junk. (But then, you don't have to interpret such claims *that* way at all, and I don't see how anyone sensible can if they are to understand what Marx was really about. Still, again, it would be irrelevant to pursue the point here.)

Finally – my third observation – I think readers will agree with me that liberalism is a prevailing orthodoxy. Arguably, it is *the* prevailing orthodoxy. At any rate, it is my guess that the majority of those who read this are, in fact, liberals in the sense that they adhere to the four tenets listed.

In my opening paragraph, I stated my opinion that humanists should take more than a passing interest in liberalism, so, before I move on, let me explain why. I can be brief here. I shan't waste my time trying to define 'humanist' with any rigour. I shall simply take it that if you doubt the existence of God then you have satisfied one of the necessary conditions for someone's being a humanist. But there is another such condition, and that is that you must not be a Stalinist. What I mean is this: as I am sure everyone knows, Stalin's activities demonstrated that an atheistic regime can deal just as viciously with dissidents as regimes with a religiously based ideology could with heretics. When it came to uncompromisingly ruthless sadism there was really nothing to choose between the Inquisition and the Cheka. Whatever the degree of their hostility to religion may be, are there humanists who would be pre-pared to see the legal proscription of religion, the abolition of churches, mosques, synagogues, the clergy being forced to perform more useful tasks, and so on? I doubt it.

## The Problem: Is Liberalism 'Just Another Point of View'?

That said, what of the problem I said I wanted to raise? This relates to the fact that liberalism is a particular system of values, that it is – if you like – a 'world-view'. There can be no doubt about it. Before the late sixteenth and early seventeenth centuries, there was no liberalism. The known world was dominated by all-embracing religious belief systems which claimed a monopoly of both truth and justice. You believed what they said and you did what you were told – or else. It was during the later part of the sixteenth century, and in Europe, that the monopoly began to break down. In short, there was the Reformation. There were religious wars of which no-one was the outright winner. You can think of liberalism – with its emphasis on toleration and the mutual recognition of rights – as an outcome of compromises which had to be struck. Indeed, some of liberalism's earlier texts – Milton's *Areopagitica* (Milton 1974) for example, and Locke's *Letter Concerning Toleration* (Locke 1991) – are, quite specifically, arguments for *religious* toleration. It was only later that such arguments became secularised.[1]

In short, liberalism is a particular world-view that originated at a particular time in a particular part of the world. (Incidentally, this fact has to be embarrassing for the idea that we have 'human rights' simply by virtue of the fact that we are humans. If the fact of our having rights was more or less equivalent to the fact of our being featherless bipeds with relatively large brains, you would think somebody would have noticed before.) So the problem to which I would like to find an answer is this: Given that liberalism is, as I have put it, a 'world-view', what makes it any better than, or different from, any other world-view?

Let me put it another way. It has occasionally been put to me that I 'only' believe in free speech, or rights, 'because I am a liberal', rather as if 'being a liberal' is rather like 'being a Catholic' or 'being an Arsenal supporter'. How am I to respond? The trouble is that, given what I have been saying, being a liberal is in some ways exactly parallel to being an Arsenal supporter. For example, if you are an Arsenal supporter, your enthusiasm for the team is more likely than not to originate in the fact that you inhabit a particular locality (North London). Likewise – (likewise?) – if you are a liberal it is probable that you are a Westerner living some time after 1690 (the year in which Locke's *Second Treatise* was published). What I want to say is that my liberalism is, somehow, of a different order from other belief-systems (the Arsenal supporter's, religious and political beliefs of various kinds); that it undercuts them; that it is more fundamental. But can I say such things?

That may not be a happy, or precise, way to phrase the problem, but at present it's the best I can think of. Rather than struggle further, let me place it in the context of an example. Consider, then, the destruction of the Great Library at Alexandria. The library had existed since classical times and was said to preserve 'all the knowledge in the world'. However, when Egypt was conquered by the Arabs in AD 640 it was razed to the ground by fire. Legend has it that this was done on the instructions of the Caliph. The story could well be apocryphal,[2] but from the point of view of my question that does not matter. What matters is that the Caliph is said to have reasoned as follows: 'these books will either contradict the Koran, in which case they are heresy, or they will agree with it, so they are superfluous'. The website, from which I have gleaned this information, adds that, 'So enormous was the volume of literature that it took six months for it all to be burnt to ashes heating the saunas of the conquerors.'[3]

It is pretty obvious that burning a library in which 'all the knowledge in the world' is supposedly preserved is an action of which no liberal can approve. (Out of the tenets I listed earlier, the second – which mentions liberty of conscience and freedom of speech and expression – would seem to be especially relevant here.) However, I think it is equally obvious that, if you look at things from the Caliph's point of view, you have to treat his action as perfectly rational. The Caliph genuinely believes that the Koran, being the Holy Book, is the source of all knowledge and wisdom. If he is right, then it follows, as he claims, that the existence of the books is either offensive or pointless and that there is – at the very least – no good reason for not destroying the library. (So, why not use them for heating the saunas of the city?) If liberalism is 'just another point of view' the story should end here. If you are happy with that, fine. If not, now suppose that you are back in AD 640, just prior to the event, and that, as a liberal – assuming that you are one – you have a chance to dissuade the Caliph from destroying the library. What would you say?

It isn't easy to come up with a satisfactory answer. For example, it is likely that many readers will want to challenge the Caliph by questioning his premise. They will say that the Caliph's belief is an irrational superstition. More specifically, they will insist that there is no such thing as a holy book in which all knowledge and wisdom is contained and, therefore, that the Caliph's reason for burning the library is a bad one. But this would be the wrong response, even though the Caliph's premise is, indeed, just as false as this response assumes.

There are two reasons why. The first is that, in responding that way you would be responding as an atheist, whereas what we are seeking is the response it would be appropriate for a liberal to give. To see the difference, you need only note that, in the former case, your response is consistent with your thinking it acceptable to burn all the 'superstitious' books the library contains should you find yourself in the Caliph's position. (Just as he reasons that it is pointless to preserve heresy, so might you reason that it is pointless to preserve superstition. This being the seventh century AD, you would probably end up burning the whole library, just as he did.)

The second is that it's boring. With the response in question, either you will fail to persuade the Caliph to adopt your own point of view or you will succeed. If you fail, you will have got no further. If you succeed you will have done just that – succeeded in persuading him to adopt your point of view. That's boring because it's just obviously, tautologically, true that someone who shares your point of view will agree with you. Against this, what we are seeking is a reason which both the atheist and the Caliph – being rational individuals – can recognise as a reason for *not* burning the library, while at the same time retaining their respective – and quite separate – attitudes to religion.

To this, I should add that I would like to find something more than a reason that the two of you can recognise as such merely because you happen to be the individuals you are. For example, there will be such a reason if it should turn out that you both like reading books. (Why burn the library and deprive yourselves of so much pleasure?) Because it appeals to a preference, and not to an ethical principle, this would be far too 'local' to be the reason I am seeking. Again, it could turn out that neither of you is so powerful that you can ignore the other's demands. Some sort of *modus vivendi* has to be established, so you reach some sort of compromise. This reason is both too local and too pragmatic.

At this point, it may help if I summarise the situation, as I have presented it so far as follows. You could say that there are three distinct 'perspectives' or 'points of view' at issue here. One is that of the religious fundamentalist, the Caliph. From his perspective, the destruction of the library is rational if it contains nothing but heresy or work which simply reiterates the Koran. Another is that of the illiberal, intolerant, atheist. From this point of view, it is quite rational to destroy the library if it contains nothing but superstition. Third, there is the liberal perspective. From this standpoint, destroying the library is wantonly wrong. Now, what I want to find is a persuasive reason why the third of these is genuinely superior to the other two, so much so that it – so to speak – 'trumps' them.

What if there turns out to be no such reason? Well, I will then have to accept that each perspective exists 'on a level' with the others. This will mean resigning myself to a sort of moral relativism, according to which things that appear right from one perspective may appear wrong from another, so much so that how you view them will only depend on where you happen to be standing. If this is right, not only can there be no *absolute* standard against which the merits of some perspectives can be judged, there can't even be standards which, if not absolute, are at least better than others.

To this, I should add the following. Having reached this point, I realise that some readers will want to accuse me of pursuing a chimera. They will insist that there can be no absolute standard against which others can be measured; that the idea that there can be is an over-optimistic 'foundationalist' myth. Postmodernists and their like will want to add that, by trying to put morality on a rational foundation, I am hopelessly in pursuit of the 'Enlightenment project', as if the 'Enlightenment project' were a rusty toy locomotive, and those who pursue it superannuated trainspotters, trying in vain to set it going. In reply, I should say, first, that I have nothing against the Enlightenment, or rationality. (In fact, I am quite a fan of both.) However, second, as it happens I am not committed to a belief in the existence of an absolute, 'foundational', standard. All I am committed to is the belief that some standards are more authoritative, and in that sense 'deeper', than others. That has to be the case if liberalism is to be a coherent world-view. (There may be such a thing as an absolute standard. I haven't made my mind up about that yet. Here, the point is that my argument does not commit me to a belief in it. At present, my feeling is that the absolute/relative dichotomy is too stark to do justice to conceptual realities in this area. It's more likely to be a question of degrees – of more and less. Still, that's another story.)

Finally, I should add that – of course – the problem I have just described is not something I have just invented or thought up. On the contrary, it has been addressed by a number of philosophers, and I shall discuss some contemporary solutions in a moment. Before I do, let me just say why I believe it is a problem to be taken seriously, and not just the sort of conundrum philosophers like to amuse themselves with in their spare time.

The factor that ensures that the issue I am addressing here is a real and urgent one is that we are, as never before, constrained to share the planet with others who pursue lifestyles, hold world-pictures, and adhere to value-systems that are very different from our own. Consider: modern communications are such that information in an easily comprehensible written or pictorial form can be transmitted right across the world more or less instantaneously. Not only that, but people can move much more easily from one part of the globe to another: there is now no advanced country which is not multi-ethnic, multi-faith, multi-cultural. It is no longer realistic to think that there can be a single religious belief-system to which everyone living in a given geographical area is committed (as would have been the norm in pre-Reformation times). It is no longer possible to think of the Earth's resources as limitless. We have to share them. The world's economy is increasingly dominated by multinational corporations, whose activities affect us all but are beyond the control of individual national governments. And so on.

I have compiled the list in a fairly random, 'off the top of the head' manner, and I could continue it. Still, it is long enough, and – as it is becoming rather commonplace for writers on contemporary affairs to draw our attention to such facts – I shan't. I think everyone here will be familiar with the rough, rather 'catch-all', phrases with which such facts, or subsets of them, tend to be categorised – 'globalisation', 'pluralism', and suchlike. Now, if there is such a thing as 'the problem of pluralism' then liberalism – with its emphasis on toleration – is uniquely placed to solve it at the philosophical level. Therefore, there are compelling reasons for taking liberalism seriously. Of course, it may turn out that no solution is possible – if you like, that a preference for liberalism is no less local than the Caliph's taste for reading which, as I hypothesised a moment ago, could have been appealed to in order to dissuade him from burning the library. Let us now consider some potential answers.

## Solutions?

Let me just summarise the position we have now reached. We are seeking a principle (or principles) from which a liberal value-system can be derived, and which satisfies the following criteria: (i) It must be more than 'local' in its appeal (that is, it must do more than invoke considerations which 'just happen' to be persuasive so far as the particular individuals to whom it is addressed in a given instance are concerned). (ii) It must be more than pragmatic (i.e. something people accept, simply out of the need to establish a *modus vivendi*). (iii) It must apply, whether or not it is accepted as a good reason by the parties to whom it is addressed (that is, it must entail that the Caliph ought not to have the library burnt, even if it should transpire that he goes ahead and has it burnt anyway). This last criterion arises from the fact that we are seeking ethical principles here – a set of standards to which human behaviour ought to conform.

So, a non-local non-pragmatic principle (or set of principles) that everyone ought to recognise – can there really be such a thing? It looks like a tall order. In what follows, I shall briefly consider three possible sources of a solution: first, the contractualist approach taken by John Rawls; second, what I shall call 'the argument from radical uncertainty' (early versions of which can be found in Locke and Mill); third, the 'postmodernist' or 'revisionist' liberalism of Richard Rorty.

I will take Rawls first because his 'contractualist' approach offers by far the most promising hope of a solution to my present difficulty. More than that, I am sure that a great many readers will agree with me that Rawls's political philosophy is by far the most imaginative and the most serious to have been produced in the last half-century. As I am sure many readers will know already, Rawls's work is centred upon a thought experiment. We are invited to imagine a group of individuals in a hypothetical situation – 'the original position' – from which they choose principles that set the terms upon which they co-operate. Various restrictions are placed upon the way the original position is set up. These are meant to reflect certain aspects of the concept of justice – so that there can be no arbitrary bias, for example – as well as aspects of the human condition itself. (For example, it is supposed that people stand to gain through co-operating with each other.) According to Rawls, the principles so chosen are the principles of justice in terms of which we can evaluate real-life social and political practices. As Rawls sees it, the thought experiment is meant to reflect the 'pluralistic' reality of the modern human situation. That is what makes his work so serious.

As I am sure readers will also know, Rawls's original thesis has undergone a number of modifications and revisions. It has also generated an enormous amount of critical commentary. I can only be brief here, and there would be absolutely no point in my trying to add to the material which already exists, so I will just state my opinion that the jury is still out on Rawls (and on the contractualist approach generally). The reason is that, so far as I can see, it is one thing to specify terms of co-operation and quite another to defend the liberal values specified in the tenets I listed at the beginning of this piece. Rawls's contractualist model will certainly yield principles to which, given certain assumptions, everyone will agree, but it is by no means clear that he can derive a fully fledged liberal value-system from the same principles. That is what he sets out to do but – for reasons I don't have the time to spell out here – I am not convinced that he succeeds.

Where the contractualist approach argues, in effect, that liberalism is an ethically reasonable response to pluralism and disagreement, my second solution – that from 'radical uncertainty' – takes a more practical, this-worldly approach, by pointing to freedom's practical benefits. One example – the best known – is provided by Mill's argument, in chapter 2 of *On Liberty*, that liberty of thought and discussion serves to facilitate the discovery of truth and, in its turn, the progress of civilisation. In essence, it is Mill's argument that, 'since the general or prevailing opinion on any subject is rarely or never the whole truth, it is only by the collision of adverse opinions that the remainder of the truth has any chance of being supplied' (1991: 59). In chapter 3, he offers a parallel argument for 'individuality': namely that the greatest happiness principle requires that people should be left free to conduct 'experiments in living'.

A word of warning is in order here. Since its publication in 1859, Mill's *On Liberty* has remained the most widely known, widely appealed to, defence of liberalism there is. Like Shakespeare's work, it is the source of many powerful aphorisms: 'The only purpose for which power can be rightfully exercised ... is to prevent harm to others' (ibid.: 14); 'There is a sphere of action in which society, as distinguished from the individual, has, if any, only an indirect interest' (ibid.: 16); 'If all mankind minus one were of one opinion, mankind would be no more justified in silencing that one person than he, if he had the power, would be justified in silencing mankind' (ibid.: 21); 'All silencing of discussion is an assumption of infallibility' (ibid.: 22). Such resounding phrases are familiar to every journalist who has ever written in defence of (what he or she believes to be) toleration or free speech – including every such journalist who has never read *On Liberty* or even heard of John Stuart Mill. Mill's argument is, in fact, quite powerful, but there can be a lazy tendency to rely upon it in all cases without being aware of its defects. It is essential to avoid this.

Just briefly, the main problem with Mill's positive arguments is that they hold only for a certain range of cases; that is, cases for which it is (contingently) true that the exercise of the liberties he sets out to defend really does have the effects he claims. This range may be more limited than a fully fledged liberal value-system requires. Take his argument for the liberty of thought and discussion as a case in point. This works fine where the truth is unknown, and especially well where it is unknowable. That is why it works very well as a defence of religious toleration. By definition, none of us knows what awaits us beyond that bourne from which no traveller returns. So we may as well be left free to tolerate each other's opinions on the subject. (That is why I have called it 'the argument from radical uncertainty'.) By contrast, what are the implications of Mill's argument for, say, the literature of Holocaust denial? You would have to possess a wilful disregard for evidence to deny that the Holocaust ever took place, or that Auschwitz was an extermination camp. (For a start, if taken there, and shown the gas chambers and the museum, you would have to insist that, even so, it was not an extermination camp.) In this case, it's difficult to know what purpose could be served, in most circumstances, by permitting liberty of thought and discussion on this point – as if it were a question of philosophy, politics, or theoretical physics – especially when the effects of the exercise of such a liberty could be detrimental. Or, what if an 'experiment in living' simply leads to a life of addiction and crime?

Well, that is the central problem with Mill's argument – and I am sure many readers will find it familiar. I am also sure that, faced with this type of objection, Mill would have produced plenty of responses from up his sleeve. The argument certainly doesn't end there.[4] However, this is not the right place to pursue it further, so let me turn, instead, to the third item on my list, Rorty's defence of liberalism – his 'revisionist' defence, as I have labelled it.

Richard Rorty's distinctive contribution to philosophy is his 'ironism'; an 'ironist' being someone who realises 'that anything can be made to look good or bad by being redescribed' (Rorty 1989: 73). On this account, it is a mistake to think that disagreements can necessarily be settled by an appeal to some objective standard – 'rational', 'foundational', or whatever. Argument and discussion are more a question of persuasion – of answering a description with a redescription, a redescription with a re-redescription, and so on. What has this to do with liberalism? Rorty's answer is that 'It is central to the idea of a liberal society that, in respect to words as opposed to deeds, persuasion as opposed to force, anything goes' (ibid.: 51). A liberal society is, thus, a society whose institutions are designed to facilitate free discussion and interchange – and that's it. Thus, according to Rorty, '*A liberal society is one which is content to call "true" whatever the upshot of such encounters turns out to be*' (ibid.: Rorty's emphasis).

Clearly, it is an implication of this account of liberalism that my search for a principle from which a liberal value-system can be derived is pointless. In a way, this makes it quite attractive. If Rorty is right, at least I can give up and relax.

Even so, as far as I can see there is plenty wrong with Rorty's argument. For one thing, it doesn't seem to explain *why* the process of answering descriptions with re-descriptions should be encouraged and allowed to continue. What's so great about it? Is it simply that it's fun? Is it that human progress requires it? If neither of these, then what? Either Rorty leaves such questions unanswered or we are back to the search for a principle. At least, that is how it seems to me.

Still, rather than dwell on that point, I will mention just one other: Rorty, by replacing the notion of an appeal to rationality with the notion of persuasion, undermines his own liberalism. If persuasion is what counts then how can Rorty distinguish (i) persuading someone to accept one's point of view by appealing to 'objective' principles of logic from (ii) persuading the other person by redescribing something to make it look good or bad; from (iii) getting that person to accept it by surreptitiously appealing to his/her greed or vanity; from (iv) using subliminal advertising techniques to sell one's argument; from (v) using drugs or hypnosis for the same purpose? Presumably Rorty would not allow the final item on this list but, if persuasion is all, where exactly does he draw the line? For Rorty, the problem is that the later items on the list – even, perhaps, the items from (ii) onwards – are means for undermining the *autonomy* of the other person. That is, when you surreptitiously appeal to someone's greed or vanity, or subject them to subliminal advertising techniques, you *manipulate* them.

The consequence for Rorty's liberalism is just this. A liberalism founded upon his 'ironist' account of disagreement could not maintain both that there are rights to freedom of speech and discussion, or to live one's life in one's own way, and at the same time found this right in an account of human freedom construed as autonomy. The second and the fourth tenets listed at the opening of this piece would come into contradiction with each other. So, if this is liberalism, it is liberalism *manqué*, and logically broken-backed.

So, where does this leave us? The possibilities are: (i) that there is a solution to the problem I have been discussing here; (ii) that the only possible solutions are pragmatic rather than philosophical; and (iii) that I am mistaken in thinking there is a problem at all – in other words that it is a non-problem. Perhaps time will tell. For myself, I continue to believe that liberty is pretty important, perhaps even 'sacred', and I continue to live in hope.

## Notes

1  I argue the point at length in Part One of my *Free Speech* (Haworth 1998).
2  According to some accounts, the story is piece of Crusader propaganda, designed to cast the other side in a disreputable light.
3  The website address is *http://www.bede.org.uk/library.htm*.
4  For a start, defenders of Mill can argue that where the short-term consequences of the exercise of liberty of expression apparently contradict his case, these are outweighed by long-term consequences. Clearly, there is a lot more to be said, on either side, than I can say here.

## References

Haworth, Alan (1998) *Free Speech*, London: Routledge.
Locke, John (1988) [1690] *Second Treatise of Civil Government*, in Locke, *Two Treatises of Government*, student edition, ed. Peter Laslett, Cambridge: Cambridge University Press.
Locke, John, (1991) [1689] *A Letter Concerning Toleration*, in John Horton and Susan Mendus (eds), *John Locke, 'A Letter Concerning Toleration' in Focus*, London: Routledge.
Marx, Karl and Engels, Frederick (1991) [1888] *The Communist Manifesto*, in *Marx, Engels, Selected Works*, revised edition, London: Lawrence & Wishart; New York: International Publishers.
Mill, John Stuart (1991) [1859] *On Liberty*, in John Gray (ed.), *John Stuart Mill: On Liberty and Other Essays*, Oxford: Oxford University Press.
Milton, John (1974) [1644] *Areopagitica*, in C.A. Patrides, (ed.), *John Milton: Selected Prose*, London: Penguin.

Rawls, John (1972) *A Theory of Justice*, Oxford: Clarendon Press.
Rorty, Richard (1989) *Contingency, Irony, and Solidarity*, Cambridge: Cambridge
    University Press.

# 8 The Limits of Liberty

## A response to Alan Haworth

## Michael Clark

Alan Haworth relates the story of the destruction of the Great Library at Alexandria, which was said to contain all the knowledge in the world. The Arabs who conquered Egypt set fire to the library on the instructions of the Caliph, wholly destroying it. The Caliph reasoned that a book would either be heretical because it contradicted the Koran or redundant since it agreed with it. As liberals, Haworth claims, we need a reason for not burning the library that the Caliph can accept, while we both retain our own beliefs, in particular our beliefs about religion. The reason he seeks is to be an ethical one reached by rational individuals, not merely a matter of personal preferences (we both like reading) or a compromise reached for pragmatic reasons. (Though what a compromise would look like I cannot imagine – burn some of the books, restrict library opening hours, restrict the library to elite citizens?)

But this question has no answer. The Caliph believes the Koran is the repository of all truth and is not prepared to tolerate opposition, the liberal believes in freedom of speech and expression. There is no way of reconciling the two. If the liberal tolerates the Caliph and the destruction of the library, he does not remain true to his own views. Of course he can and should allow the Caliph to express his beliefs, and to that extent he can tolerate intolerance, but he cannot tolerate the

Caliph's undermining of freedom of speech and expression by destroying the library; that would be self-defeating.

Does the liberal's intolerance faced with the Caliph mean that liberalism is just another necessarily intolerant point of view, one theory among others? No. Complete neutrality is logically precluded. When the intolerance takes the form of suppressing free speech, or takes the form of hate crimes, it must itself be suppressed, otherwise nothing is left of liberalism. But liberalism is distinctive in being maximally tolerant. So it is not true, as Haworth claims, that, if there turns out to be no reason of the sort he asks for, each perspective – liberal, religious fundamentalist, etc. – is 'on a level' with the others.

Thus, it is wrong to think, as Haworth does, that we need to evaluate Rawls or Mill in terms of how they succeed in answering his question. Wrong, because no answer could conceivably convince both the Caliph and a liberal, but wrong too, because it doesn't follow from the non-existence of an answer that liberalism is just another world-view.

Rawls and Mill do, however, give us reasons why freedom is 'hugely important' and it is to these that I now turn. (I shall say nothing of Rorty, because I accept Haworth's dismissal of his ironism.)


## Rawls

A rational political liberal needs to set aside personal dispositions to take advantage of others and unfairly invade their freedom. As Kant puts it in the *Groundwork* when he presents his supreme principle in terms of a kingdom of ends:

> since laws determine ends in terms of their universal valid-
> ity, if we abstract from the personal differences of rational
> beings as well as from the content of their private ends we

shall be able to think of a whole of all ends in systematic
connection.

(Kant 1996: 83)

John Rawls's *A Theory of Justice* found a new way of defending the
primacy of freedom by having hypothetical contractors choose rationally behind a veil of ignorance, where although you are aware of the
general character of human nature, your social status, assets, talents,
strength and personality are hidden from you, thereby removing any
motives to seek unfair advantage. Choice should be rational but self-
interested. A contractor will seek to maximise for herself those primary
goods – opportunities, wealth, income and the bases of self-respect –
that Rawls says it is rational to want whatever else you want, those
which are required for success in advancing your own ends. This is his
'original position'.

Rawls claims that those in the original position will choose two
basic principles of justice, the first of which is: 'Each person is to have
an equal right to the most extensive basic liberty compatible with a
similar liberty for others' (Rawls 1972: 60). His other principle allows
wealth and income to be unequal only when that is to everyone's
advantage, and requires positions of authority to be open to all. For
some, Rawls's position is too individualist, for others, not individualist
enough. For the communitarian such individualism risks dissolving
social bonds, which they claim depend on society's customs and traditional morality. But such a view is antagonistic to the negative liberty
Haworth and I are both concerned to defend. On the other hand, the
veil of ignorance precludes knowing about our talents, and the principles of justice that emerge do not allow for rewarding talents. But if
Rawls's position is flawed in detail, as Haworth believes it to be, is the
general approach wrong?

The contractualist approach is certainly not dead. A more relaxed, broadly Kantian framework is proposed by Thomas Scanlon in *What We Owe to Each Other*. 'What we are trying to decide is,' says Scanlon, 'first and foremost, whether certain principles are ones that no one, if suitably motivated, could reasonably reject' (Scanlon 1998: 189). Rawls's contractors are rational and self-interested, and impartiality is secured by placing them behind a veil of ignorance. Scanlon needs no rational self-interested calculation, and no veil of ignorance to secure impartiality, since others' points of view are necessarily taken into account in the search for principles they have reason to accept. (Indeed, in his later writings Rawls himself replaces 'rational' by 'reasonable'.)

Neither Rawls's nor Scanlon's hypothetical contracts are engines for generating a totality of moral principles *ab initio*. When assessing one principle we need to appeal to others which are held fixed, though they may be questioned in their turn by holding the others fixed – like Neurath's ship, which can only be repaired at sea piecemeal, by replacing some planks while standing on others, then replacing the others by standing on those just replaced. So if reasonable contractors reject a principle that restricts the liberty of some for the sake of that of others, they do not do so without relying on other principles. (Scanlon 1998: 214. Cf. Rawls's notion of reflective equilibrium, 1972: 20.)

## Mill

Even if the contractualist approach does not work, we have the powerful arguments of John Stuart Mill. Haworth complains that his 'arguments only work for a range of cases'. 'All silencing of discussion is an assumption of infallibility', says Mill (1982: 77). This is what Haworth calls the 'argument from radical uncertainty', which he claims works only when the truth is unknown. But we know for certain, for example, that Holocaust denial is false; the evidence for the Holocaust is so strong as to leave no conceivable doubt about its historicity. So he concludes that no purpose is served, 'in most circumstances', by allowing its expression and discussion.

Haworth misinterprets Mill in treating the argument from infallibility as an argument from radical uncertainty. Mill tells us that the assumption of infallibility is 'not the feeling sure of a doctrine. . . . It is the undertaking to decide the question *for others*, without allowing them to hear what can be said on the contrary side' (1982: 83). 'Reliance can be placed on [a belief] only when the means of setting it right are kept constantly in mind' (1982: 80). We need to hear the arguments against it to understand how false the denial is, otherwise it becomes a dogma we might suspect had some truth in it.

> If the cultivation of the understanding consists in one thing more than another, it is surely in learning the grounds of one's own opinions. Whatever people believe, on subjects on which it is of the first importance to believe rightly, they ought to be able to defend against at least the common objections.
>
> (1982: 97)

To ban Holocaust denial, as in Germany, would make us lose what Mill calls 'the clearer perception and livelier impression of truth produced by its collision with error' (1982: 76). Open discussion will make us more aware of the historical background and reasons for the Holocaust, and will analyse and substantiate the evidence for it. The evidence presented for the Holocaust in David Irving's recent (2000) suit against Deborah Lipstadt, who wrote a searing critique of work in which he denied the Holocaust (Lipstadt 1994), is a case in point. Irving's falsehoods and distortions were dramatically exposed. What was revealed in the trial deepened and extended our knowledge of the Holocaust, and, as one historian remarked at the time, a lot of history would be ruled out if we read only writers to whom we feel intellectually akin. There is *something* to learn even from Nazi historians.

Of course, it is different when Holocaust denial becomes a hate crime, when it seeks to stir up discontent and violence, but prohibition of such conduct falls easily under Mill's Harm Principle. As we are often told, freedom of expression does not extend to crying 'Fire!' in a crowded theatre.

Mill also extols the value of different 'experiments in living'. Here again, Haworth wrongly argues that Mill's argument is flawed because it works only for a limited range of experiments. 'What if an experiment leads to addiction and crime?', he asks. But criminal behaviour harmful to others is banned by the Harm Principle! Such conduct threatens the liberty of others and may rightly be prohibited. Mill's position is not flawed, because it is clear that it does not condone every experiment in living which harms others.

## Is Liberty Sacred?

Despite the title of his essay, and the theme of this book, Haworth does not directly address this question. So I will conclude by briefly considering it myself.

There is good reason to regard liberty as of value in itself. As a utilitarian Mill's official position was that liberty was valuable because it conduced to happiness. But liberty and happiness can surely come into conflict. Some people, for example, are more content in a con-trolled environment like the armed forces or a monastery than in freer circumstances.

But being valuable in itself does not make liberty sacred. Why? Because to say that something is sacred is to say that it is inviolable. If liberty were sacred, then no restrictions on it would be permissible, just as if life were sacred it would never be permissible to take a life, even in self-defence. Yet liberty, like life, is far from inviolable. Indeed, short of engaging in utopianism, it is impossible to imagine a society that did not violate some people's liberty some of the time. The equal liberty for all enshrined in Rawls's first principle of justice is incompatible with unlimited liberty for anyone. Similarly, Mill's Harm Principle allows the state to prohibit conduct harmful to others.

Moreover, there is a case for restricting liberty for the sake of other values. In conditions of great poverty and disease, liberty does not have the same value, and can readily be sacrificed to improve condi-tions. In happier conditions, equality can be pursued by welfare redistribution through taxation, and that limits our freedom to spend all our earnings as we wish. Any considerations in favour of this would be incompatible with the sanctity of liberty. Indeed, as libertarians would argue, if liberty were sacred it would trump everything else. Liberty, however valuable, is not sacred.

## References

Haworth, Alan (2004), 'Is Liberty Sacred?', this volume.

Kant, Immanuel (1996 [1785]) *Groundwork of the Metaphysic of Morals*, in *Practical Philosophy*, tr. and ed. Mary J. Gregor, Cambridge: Cambridge University Press.

Lipstadt, Deborah E. (1994) *Denying the Holocaust*, London: Penguin.

Mill, John Stuart (1982 [1859]) *On Liberty*, London: Penguin.

Rawls, John (1972) *A Theory of Justice*, Oxford: Clarendon Press.

Scanlon, Thomas (1998) *What We Owe to Each Other*, Cambridge, Mass. and London: Belknap Press.

# 9   The Idea of the Sacred

## Piers Benn

The essays in this collection have discussed whether anything is sacred, but the word 'sacred' tends to be used quite loosely. Sometimes it appears to mean little more than 'very valuable'. Thus when people ask whether art or liberty are sacred, often they are really asking whether these things should be highly valued, never to be compromised for the sake of something else. At other times the word is used with religious overtones, invoking that before which we should stand in fear and trembling, or alternatively things that are absolutely inviolable and must be protected at all costs, perhaps because they are created and loved by God. This is the idea behind the sanctity of human life; we are not gods, but our lives are held to be sacred because we are made in God's image. Indeed, the 'sanctity' of human life, even if such an idea is misconceived, has a moral resonance that is lacking in lame and woolly talk of the 'value' of human life.

It seems to me that the subject of the sacred is best approached within a religious context, since religion (or certain religions) more than anything else makes the idea of the sacred intelligible, perhaps by offering rituals, or doctrines, or an approach to life which speaks to the human condition in a way that nothing else can.

However, I start from a rather anomalous position. For reasons that may not be altogether coherent, I define myself as agnostic, rather than atheist or humanist. Perhaps because I have a fairly religious temperament but a sceptical mind, I have always found it difficult to commit myself either for or against any religious creed, though I have long been intrigued by the issue. I leave on one side the interesting debate about whether it is more rational for a non-theist to be agnostic or atheist. There are complex questions about the onus of justification with respect to theism, and the state of the evidence; questions complicated by the fact that some philosophers argue that belief in God is 'properly basic' and can be rational even in the absence of evidence. However, it is difficult to be convinced of God's existence when one considers the many philosophical objections raised, especially the Enlightenment critiques of natural theology, including David Hume's literary and philosophical masterpiece the *Dialogues Concerning Natural Religion.* And then there are the particular stumbling blocks in the way of Christianity, including doctrines of original sin, atonement, substitutionary punishment, free will and grace.

At the same time I am troubled by my agnosticism because, unlike many humanists, I think a sense of the sacred is something that it is good to have, and which we lose at our peril. Indeed, it leads us to think about other concepts, such as idolatry. If you take the sacred seriously, then it must be very important not to take the wrong things as sacred, and not to worship false gods. So when God tells the Jews that they must have no other God before Him, He is not primarily making an ontological point – saying that no other gods exist – but is stressing that His followers must not worship any other god. And the distinction between proper and improper objects of devotion can, to some extent, be given a rational and non-religious basis. The sacred must somehow speak truly and faithfully to our condition. For this reason many ethical traditions warn against the worship of money, reputation, status, or other people, because in the end these never deliver on their promises.

The idea that monotheism puts before us is that God alone is able to deliver on the promises He makes to us, and freely offers us eternal life, in which our deepest needs and desires will be fulfilled. Nothing else can do so.

But we can't ignore the question of whether we can coherently combine agnosticism, or even atheism, with this sense of the sacred; with the conviction that a sense of sacred things, suitably allied with reason, is a good thing to have. I am troubled because I am not sure one can reconcile these views. So I simply admit to something which points to a conflict and a tension within myself. Of course, one can distract oneself by shelving the question of whether anything *ought* to be considered sacred, and instead considering the matter naturalistically, devising biological, social or psychological explanations of how the idea of the sacred has arisen. Such explanations have a certain charm and plausibility, especially for debunkers. For if we can explain why certain ideas are likely to arise, even if there is no real substance to them, then their claim to truth appears to be seriously undermined.

A parallel to this is in functional explanations of certain religious obligations. The practising Jew or Muslim, for example, observes the dietary laws of his religion, regarding them as divinely ordained, and no doubt healthy and hygienic as well. But now imagine an anthropologist coming onto the scene, who notices these dietary practices and offers a theory as to their origin. Dietary restrictions, he announces, are a good way of limiting social contact with outsiders. Meals are family or social occasions, and if you can't eat the same food as outsiders, then it is relatively difficult to socialise with them. And that has a useful social function, since it greatly reduces the chances of sex with them, or intermarriage. Practising adherents of such religions may not be conscious of this functional explanation of their laws, but for our imaginary anthropologist, that is what they are really about.

To offer such explanations for religious observance, or more generally for the sense of sacred things, is in a way to adopt an external or observer's perspective upon them. The sociologist Emile Durkheim hypothesised that the early Jewish idea of God arose because of the need to cement the bonds of tribal membership. The duties owed by individuals towards others of the tribe were not based on modern ideas of a social contract, but on membership, which is not chosen, though it is a deep source of security. This membership needs a focal point that commands unquestioning loyalty, and which somehow represents the spirit of the community. The idea of God, with associated sacred rituals, came to be that focal point. Obligations are justified by reference to the will of a being far more powerful and wise than ourselves, and who takes an active interest in the tribe's affairs. Again, if we believe Durkheim's account of the origin and function of religion, we may end up feeling that religion and the sacred have been debunked: *this* is really what is happening, and if people only saw this, their self-sacrificing loyalty to the community would not survive for long. The external perspective comes to be equated with a uniquely correct grasp of the reality. The internal or *participant* point of view depends upon a mistaken view of its own origins.

Hence somebody trying to hold on to the sense of the sacred from a participant or first personal perspective, as one who experiences or apprehends certain things as sacred, may have considerable difficulty reconciling that sense with the external perspective. Similarly, the idea that the impulse to worship simply arises from our psychology and our evolutionary past has a debunking or explaining-away feel to it. But the great question is whether the two are really in conflict, or only seem to be.

A similar question might be raised about moral values, though many people, including many humanists, would deny the analogy with the sacred. Simon Blackburn is known for developing an interesting theory of moral truth that he calls *quasi-realism*: the view that although there is no metaphysical moral reality, no moral facts 'out there' (whatever that might mean) that are needed to explain our moral reactions, nonetheless it is not irrational or mistaken to talk of moral claims as being true or false, justified or unjustified. Thus we can speak of moral truth, and a kind of moral objectivity, without being moral realists. Our activity of valuing things, of praising and blaming and so on, have entirely naturalistic explanations, but that doesn't show that morality has been debunked. As Blackburn has suggested, we who moralise should feel 'bunked' and not debunked.

Can one be quasi-realist with regard to the sacred? Well, perhaps one can, but it is not quite so clear. For quasi-realism to get going, there must be some supposedly extravagant doctrine that is being rejected, combined with an assurance that this rejection has no implications for the legitimacy of certain ways of speaking, since that legitimacy does not really depend upon what is denied. In the case of morality, what quasi-realism denies is moral realism. What would be denied by quasi-realism about the sacred? Perhaps some claim such as that sacredness or sanctity is an 'objective property' of sacred things, that it is part of the objective constitution of things. And we can make sense of this, if we emphasise that our experience of the sacred essentially involves an affective response, such as a feeling of awe or reverence, and not (merely) belief. But when it comes to other convictions, such as that there is a God, quasi-realism has a harder time. To be quasi-realist about God would apparently amount to saying that although there isn't a God, there's nothing wrong with talking as if there were. Perhaps the idea of God would be a 'subjective ideal' (as the 'sea of faith' theologian Don Cupitt once put it), or a way of seeing the world as suffused with grace and meaning. Indeed, it could be what I – as an agnostic who sympathises with the idea of the sacred – need for my view to be coherent. But whatever the merits of this stance – and it is attractive – real theists are surely saying something more definite. They think there really is a divine creator and judge, not just that it is vaguely legitimate to talk as if there were.

Moreover, any such quasi-realist approach would be rather different from the more popular view that the sense of the sacred is valuable because it is socially useful, or has good behavioural consequences. There is a well-known philosopher who, in conversation, was once sincerely defending the sacred, but who then said that he also believed in the Noble Lie, upheld in Plato's *Republic*. Some people who talk like this think that there is something genuinely important that religion alone can convey, but that – *entre nous* – literal doctrines, say about providence or miracles, don't really stand the test of rational scrutiny. However, we had better not tell that to *hoi polloi* because it would threaten their piety, which hinges on such beliefs. There could be reason to make claims about the sacred whilst admitting that it is just socially useful to do so. The trouble is that what is a reason to *state* something is not always a reason to *believe* something.

There is another way to understand the sense of the sacred, which follows on from what has been said but has less of a cynical air. This is that it acts as a brake on *hubris*, which is a vice whether or not any religion is true. *Hubris* involves the arrogant over-stepping of boundaries, sometimes described as 'playing God', though many who use that phrase are somewhat vague as to how literally they mean it. Some stances within the environmental movement are rooted in the fear of *hubris*. Commonly voiced objections to genetically modified organisms, for example, are ostensibly about the empirical dangers they pose, but are really motivated by something deeper and harder to articulate. Indeed, it is because they are so hard to articulate that debate shifts to empirical matters instead, as a kind of smokescreen. Equally, strongly held objections to reproductive cloning, genetic enhancement and some new reproductive technologies are often fuelled by similar fears. Officially the talk is of the possibly appalling consequences of such technology, but very often the underlying horror is a sense that sacred things, understood religiously or not, are violated by such developments. How else can the vehemence of the reaction be explained?

If this is correct, we need to examine the relationship between a sense of the sacred and a fear of *hubris* more closely. A reasonable secular worry is that we may become over-confident of our abilities, too ready to behave with contempt towards people who resist the march of progress, and that as a result we shall make ghastly miscalculations with terrible consequences. This is one way to understand worries about, for instance, biotechnology. There is reason to believe, for example, that attempts to clone humans would be dangerous and would probably result in grossly deformed babies. That gives us good reason not to make the attempt, especially considering that cloning brings no benefits of comparable significance. But if we went ahead with it, and produced children with severe birth defects that directly resulted from the technology, much of the resulting outrage would be phrased in the language of the sacred, rather than simply being a matter of regretting the effects on the babies. Many people wouldn't say: 'These birth defects are rather unfortunate, so let's try to perfect the technology so we get it right next time.' They would say that the attempt should never even have been contemplated, and perhaps that the children's deformities are a *sign* of the deep evil of *hubris*, shown in the willingness to apply technology to 'manufacture' human life.

But the two moral stances in question, the one warning us of the empirical dangers of dabbling in things we don't fully understand, and the other warning us that such dabbling is not only unsafe but a sign of

impiety and lack of a sense of sacred things, are of course quite different. The concept of *hubris* is flexible enough to encompass both, but
the fundamental ideas are not the same. Those who take a relatively
progressive attitude to biotechnology accept that caution is wise, but see
no principled objection to the procedures in question and regard appeals
to the sacred – e.g. the sanctity of human life – as reactionary and superstitious. And they do have a point, for how do the empirical dangers of a
technological advance show that it is wrong or vicious *in principle*?

A promising answer is to admit that there is indeed no logical
connection between the riskiness of a radical technological innovation
and its being wrong in principle. However, unless we are disposed to
regard certain technologies as simply not an option, we are almost
certain to make rash and dangerous decisions. For that is just what we
are like. Constraints on our behaviour must present themselves as absolutely inviolable if they are to be effective. To reject *hubris* and to have a
sense of piety – for want of a better expression – is to be conscious of
our limitations in power and wisdom, and of the sheer fragility of our
lives and all that we care for.

We can have this sense whether or not we believe in God. If we
place our faith in an omnipotent and loving Creator, then we shall
indeed feel entitled to an ultimate hope that is denied the atheist. At the
same time, the extraordinary cruelties of the world cannot be ignored
even on the theistic view, and we face the awesome problem of evil, for
which no 'solution' seems wholly persuasive. And there are times when
an inscrutable divine will offers little more comfort than no divine will.
If we do not believe in God, then for all the humanist bravado about
facing up honestly to our condition and being as good and happy as we
can, we cannot hope that in the end all shall be well, and we should
have a heightened sense of our fragility. We should remind ourselves
that the amazing coherence and order that we experience, especially the

fact that we can know and understand things, is no sign of an underlying purpose. The idea that reality understands itself through and through, which in a way is at the heart of theism, would have to be abandoned. And none of our efforts can replace what is lost by this.

The sense of the sacred; awe in the face of an inscrutable universe; the sense that certain actions are off-limits – these are admittedly rather different notions, and I have perhaps failed to make some important distinctions. Yet these ideas share something in common, which is that they operate to guard against the excesses of human folly and vice. But even this does not resolve the earlier problem of whether anything really is sacred, as understood from a participant perspective, or whether it is just that a sense of the sacred yields good consequences for us. These positions are not incompatible, but they are different. It is hard to apprehend the sacred from the participant perspective, at the same time as admitting that the only point in doing so is to guard against the consequences of too much confidence in human power and wisdom. As mentioned earlier, if that is all there is to it, what distinctive thought is offered by the participant perspective?

I have highlighted the tension I feel about this question and can offer no definitive answer to it. An 'enchanted' world, where certain appearances are taken at their face value and where we are not always looking for their underlying explanations, is, in many ways, conducive to human contentment. Yet we should remember that such enchantment can also lead to oppression, as when we appeal to charming myths to justify the subordination of certain classes of people. We cannot do without rational reflection when working out the proper balance, but the aim should be reflective equilibrium between the sense of the sacred and other aspects of the human good, rather than triumphantly jettisoning the former in favour of what may turn out to be illusions of progress.

# 10   Salvaging the Sacred

## Simon Blackburn

A reference to the thesaurus will quickly reveal that that the word 'sacred' has religious, semi-religious and non-religious cognates. It can mean holy and blessed, or worthy of awe and reverence. One of the challenges facing humanism is to convince people that things can be worthy of awe and reverence, without being holy and blessed.

For it has to be acknowledged that in the public arena 'humanism' is itself likely to suffer from associations with spiritual poverty, or with a kind of crass, perhaps utilitarian, 'rationalistic' or 'materialistic' attitude to life. It is natural enough, of course, that religious leaders should want to hurl accusations like this, keeping the good things for themselves, denying that anybody can really plumb the spiritual depths as they do. So one can expect propaganda on this front. And that makes it doubly important to know how to fight back.

I was vividly reminded of this by a dreadful 'Thought for the Day' programme some time ago, when the speaker, who professed to be a philosopher at Wadham College, Oxford, addressed the terrible murder of two young girls at Soham in Cambridgeshire. Freely acknowledging that Christianity contained no words adequate to come to terms with such a tragedy, or to console the grieving family, he nevertheless asserted that Christian silence was a better, deeper, more adequate silence than any which an agnostic or atheist could manage. This barefaced claim to spiritual high ground needs resisting.

One resisting thought, at least, might be that voiced by Ivan in *The Brothers Karamazov* and developed by George Steiner in his book *The Death of Tragedy*, that Christianity really excludes tragedy, since it assures its followers that everything will be all right in the end.[1] Ivan cites the terrible cruelty of a landowner setting his hounds on a child, in front of the child's mother, for some minor misdemeanour, and rightly says that he does not want everything to be all right in the end. Neither man nor God has any business forgiving such an act. Similarly, to see an event such as the murder at Soham as just another manifestation of the all-powerful, all-knowing, all-good design, is to fail to find adequate horror or despair at the human nature responsible, or for that matter adequate compassion for its victims. We can turn the tables on the religious sensibility here. Just as it has always licensed untold cruelties to heretics and apostates and infidels, so it licenses something approaching stark insensibility to the evils of the world. Far from being a deeper, more profound silence than that of the humanist, the religious silence may simply express complacency or fatalism, a complicity in each and every working of divine providence.

Of course, in ordinary people things are not usually so bad. I am not suggesting that religious people do not feel compassion and grief, but just that they do this in spite of their alleged beliefs rather than because of them.

Despite being an atheist, I find a lot of things arouse a sense of the sacred in me. Works of art or music, sublime grand spectacles in nature, the starry heavens above and the moral law within, the oldest human skulls in Kenya or the newest human baby in a maternity ward can all be fitting objects of different kinds of awe and reverence. They can all take us outside ourselves. Furthermore these emotions have a moral dimension, in that we may well feel uncomfortable with some-one for whom they had no such effect. It is different, of course, if you are professionally habituated to them. We can understand the guide who works every day at the Grand Canyon, or the curator who keeps the skulls, becoming relatively indifferent through such habituation. We can understand people whose constant professional exposure or whose other cares and woes crowd out the emotional response we would expect from others. But in all such cases, the lack of response needs an excuse. Kant puzzled over the fact that the judgement that a thing is beautiful is 'demanded' of others, treated in other words as more than an idiosyncratic, personal response.[2] 'Demanded' may be slightly too strong, but it points in an important direction. It is hard to feel on all fours with someone who, dry-eyed and indifferent, is unmoved by the first sight of the Grand Canyon. We do not want gush and sentimentality, but neither do we want Stoic insensibility.

Thus Kant wrote that aesthetic taste is, in the ultimate analysis, 'a critical faculty that judges of the rendering of moral ideas in terms of sense'.[3] An idea of one's own place in the scheme of things, whether as insignificant in space and time, or as only one person amongst others, or as someone who feels as others feel, or will die as others have died, is a moral idea. Its sensual expression in nature or art is the proper object of this critical faculty. Someone who makes no response to such an expression is someone we fear to be morally deficient, disconnected and devoid of proper humanity.

Seen this way, a humanist should not feel guilty at the emotions of awe and reverence that can be inspired by great religious works of art. Religions are after all human productions, and any human response to life and death, birth and loss, touches us all. I read somewhere that Edward Gibbon wrote of a journey past Chartres words to the effect: 'I paused only to dart a look of contempt at the stately pile of superstition and passed on.' At the risk of offending more militant humanists, this strikes me as a deplorable lapse of judgement. Gibbon is quite within his rights to have no respect for the *beliefs* of the people who built Chartres. Many of those beliefs were no doubt the merest superstition. But the work shows other qualities of human beings than their beliefs. Most obviously it shows skill, knowledge, single-mindedness, a high emotional sensibility, a strong sense of virtue, of learning, and of the perhaps simple loyalty to a set of parables about how to live. It renders moral ideas in terms of sense, and it is a deficiency to let an ideological difference destroy any respect for that. Shah Jehan's tomb to his wife, the Taj Mahal, connects us through time with a sublime expression of loss, and response to loss, that has nothing to do with the organised religion of the Mughals. Meditating on what they built we can feel connected with, and in many ways envious of, them. If it is a choice between belonging to a culture which could produce the statues and windows of Chartres, and belonging to one whose supreme artistic expression is a pair of soiled underpants or the Disneyfied plastic rubbish with which the government filled the millennial dome, we do well to pause.

Richard Dawkins has complained of the tendency to see disrespect for religion as somehow bad manners. I find myself going only part of the way with Dawkins here. I find many religious beliefs as risible as he does, and feel the reverse of respect for anybody simply because they hold them. Many attitudes fostered by religions – separatism and hatred, intolerance and self-righteousness – merit contempt and even hatred. On the other hand, many, perhaps most, moving literary, architectural, musical, and artistic productions have a religious character – and we have to be careful to ensure that our well-grounded hostility to religious thinking does not blunt our response to these. To the extent that religions give voice to the emotions of other men and women –

fears, hopes, inspirations, losses and triumphs – they deserve respect. When, like English parish churches, religious artefacts do something to transmit these voices through the ages, connecting us with our own ancestors and our own landscapes, they deserve some part of the same respect that humanity deserves.

What then of the downside of the idea of the sacred? The dictionary gives us a lead, describing a sacred cow as 'a person, institution, idea etc. unreasonably held to be above questioning or criticism'. The word 'unreasonably' alerts us to the contrast class of things that are reasonably held to be above questioning or criticism.

Beyond the issue of whether atheists can properly be entitled to describe, or even experience, things as sacred, awe-inspiring or wonderful, there lurks a more difficult question about whether we have the right to view anything as deserving of unconditional commitment or allegiance. If we can't feel absolutely confident in any principles, then the question 'Is nothing sacred?' gets an affirmative answer. On such a view, there is nothing untouchable. Our loyalties must always be conditional. There is no absolute given. The view seems particularly hard to answer in moral philosophy, where simple principles and certainties so quickly collapse into a morass of distinctions and qualifications. Life is sacred, certainly. But what about just wars, criminal codes, euthanasia, self-sacrifice, suicide, and all the other conundrums, where respect for life comes up against other things with an equal claim on our loyalties? There are no foundations, exempt from critical attention, no axioms, no institutions or ideas of whose merits we are right to be uncritically convinced.

Many philosophers will endorse such a universal fallibilism. It fits with the restless, iconoclastic spirit of our age. It is indeed, almost itself a dogma, a sacred cow, of modern epistemology and moral philosophy. For at least fifty years, anti-foundationalism has triumphed. The ruling metaphor is that of Neurath's boat, of which every part can be prodded and inspected, and if necessary hauled out and replaced, all while the vessel is at sea. There is no dogma so untouchable, so sacred, as to be exempt from critical questioning. Our tribe has no idols.

Although ubiquitous, this attitude has itself had its critics, including two of the most acute minds of the last century, R. G. Collingwood, and Ludwig Wittgenstein.[4] Each doubted the possibility that critical questioning can sensibly be directed at some kinds of thoughts. We can find no standpoint from which to conduct this alleged critical thinking. For Wittgenstein some propositions, such as 'motor cars do not grow on trees' had this status.[5] An attempt to 'stand somewhere else' and think about whether it might not be true that motor cars grow on trees, cannot be sincere or real, since there is nowhere to go. That motor cars do not grow on trees is, as it were, structurally so entrenched in our form of life or our world-view that if it goes, everything goes with it. Any purported critical attitude or questioning would therefore be a kind of sham. It becomes rather like a rule of grammar, never itself in question, but determining the way other, real, inquiries are framed.

Collingwood was more interested in the metaphysical foundations of our way of thought at any particular historical juncture. With an acute sense of history, he thought that the strange and new principles of one time fossilised into the absolute metaphysical presuppositions of another time, in turn due to be retired as change goes on. The catch is that the absolute presuppositions of one time are invisible to its contemporaries. There is a kind of blindspot in the foundation of our thinking, and only history will reveal what lies within it. What lay in the medieval blindspot was the universal reach and operation of divine benevolence. What lies inside ours is, inevitably, invisible to us. But reflecting on how we behave we can, as it were, triangulate on it. Faith in what works, in the uniformity of nature, in our capacity to control our futures may seem to future historians to have marked our times more powerfully than we know.

These are abstract themes, and may seem not to connect with our more mundane moral and political problems, and particularly with the challenge we face when people hold what we believe to be the wrong things sacred. I am not so sure. The first step in engaging with our adversaries is to understand them. A Christian who believes in the Virgin Birth or a Muslim who believes that a woman is worth only four-fifths of a man may seem, to most humanists, so far beyond the pale, so utterly alien, as to be either uninterpretable, or at best an object of Gibbon-like contempt. But one step on the way to seeing how anybody *could* think such things – something that we all ought to find difficult – may be to reflect on the articles of faith buried within our own modern world-view.

We have only two options in trying to come to terms with the Other. One is understanding and dialogue, and the other is management and force. It is surely the path of humanism to prefer the first.

## Notes

1 Fyodor Dostoevsky, *The Brothers Karamazov*, trans. David McDuff, London and New York: Penguin, 2003; George Steiner, *The Death of Tragedy*, London: Faber, 1964.

2 Kant, *Critique of Judgement*, trans. J. C. Meredith, Oxford: Oxford University Press, 1986, 'Analytic of the Beautiful', Second Moment, p. 50.

3 Ibid., 'Dialectic of Aesthetic Judgement', Appendix, p. 227.

4 R. G. Collingwood, *The Idea of History*, Oxford: Oxford University Press, 1936; Ludwig Wittgenstein, *On Certainty*, Oxford: Blackwell, 1969.

5 Wittgenstein, *On Certainty*, para. 279.

# 11   The Sacred and the Scientist

## Richard Dawkins

I am pleased to have been provoked into thinking about atheism and the idea of the sacred. It's been partly an exercise in self-observation and introspection for me. I don't think they come much more anti-religious than I do. I am deeply opposed, for instance, to the existence of blasphemy laws in this country and their proposed extension. And yet there are objects and occasions which invoke in me a profound sense of the sacred, and I can cite other humanist scientists of whom this is also true.

Dr Eugene Shoemaker, the geologist after whom a famous comet is named, always wanted to be an astronaut. For various reasons he couldn't, so he spent most of his life training other people to be astronauts. When he died, his former student Caroline Porco, now a leading planetary scientist, lobbied NASA to have Shoemaker's ashes sent to the moon. And it happened. A moon shot was soon to be launched, and Shoemaker's ashes were put on board, together with a plaque bearing those famous words from Romeo and Juliet, chosen by Dr Porco for her mentor.

> And, when he shall die,
> Take him and cut him out in little stars,
> And he will make the face of heaven so fine

That all the world will be in love with night,
And pay no worship to the garish sun.

Now, call me sentimental but I was moved to tears by that story. Why?

Similarly, when I was in Kenya I went to the National Museum in Nairobi and was taken by Maeve Leakey down into the vaults to be shown the great fossils – 1470, the Turkana Boy, the Black Skull, 'Dear Boy', all these famous icons of palaeo-anthropology. On reflection it strikes me that the atmosphere was and is precisely that of a religious building. You go into these dark vaults and talk in hushed, reverential tones. The fossils are kept nested away in drawers. You are not allowed to touch them, but are given an exact replica, which you are allowed to handle. All in all, the place has a very strong and affecting sense of holiness.

Incidentally, here's a footnote to Nigel Warburton's thought experiment concerning the work of art locked up in a vault. The three-million-year-old footprints at Laetoli, in Tanzania, which were probably made by *Australopithecus afarensis* – another holy relic in my version of the sacred – having been meticulously photographed from every possible angle and mapped, have now been covered up in order to preserve them. We know they are there, and we value them being there, despite the fact that we can't experience them. (I spoil the story a bit by recognising that they can always be dug up again, and might well be dug up again when science has advanced to the point where they can be better analysed than at present.)

Another example of a scientist's sense of the sacred: I had a colleague, a distinguished neuro-physiologist. He was not a vegetarian, but a perfectly ordinary carnivore. Yet he wouldn't eat brain. He felt there was something sacrilegious about eating the brain. It was something about the complexity of it. Rationally, of course, the animal is dead, so what's the difference? But he wouldn't eat brain.

We all of us have a strong resistance to the idea of cannibalism. There really isn't any reason why one shouldn't eat road-kills but we all recoil from it. A couple of years ago, a famous gourmet called Hugh Fearnley-Whittingstall was filmed preparing and serving a dish of human placenta. He sautéed the placenta in onions, garlic and white wine and all the guests agreed that the result was delicious. Nobody realised that the placenta is a clone of the baby it nourished. Eating a human placenta is cannibalism. And I actually rather objected to that. In this case, not so much on the grounds of sacredness but on slippery slope grounds: once one breaks a powerful taboo, other things become a little easier to do. I would be against eating road-kills on the same slippery slope grounds. But I can understand that most people would think there's a kind of sacredness to human life, which would make eating a placenta or road-kill a sort of profanity.

Why, when you go to the Grand Canyon and you see the strata of geological time laid out before you, why again is there a feeling that brings you close to tears? Or looking at images from the Hubble telescope. I think it's no different from the feeling of being moved to tears by music, by a Schubert quartet, say, or by poetry. The human mind is big enough, and imaginative enough, to be poetically moved by the whole sweep of geological ages represented by the rocks that you are standing among. That's why you feel in awe. That's why you feel as though you are undergoing a religious experience when you are looking at the fossils in the Kenya National Museum. That's why when you go to Muir Woods in California, and see the cathedral spaces of the giant coast redwoods, you feel moved in a poetic way.

Poetic imagination is one of the manifestations of human nature. As scientists, and biological scientists, it's up to us to explain that, and I expect that one day we shall. And when we do explain it, it will in no way demean it. But nor should we confuse it with something supernatural.

# 12    The Concept of the Sacred
### A Response to My Critics

## Ronald Dworkin

I am delighted to have the chance to comment on the three contributions to this volume that discuss and criticise my own views about the sacred. These treat different candidates for the sacred – art, nature and human life – but they also begin in rather different views of what the sacred is.

## Nigel Warburton and the Sacred Art Object

Since Nigel Warburton believes that only objects or phenomena connected to a god can be sacred, and that there is no god, he thinks that nothing is sacred and therefore has an easy time concluding that art is not. He rejects the widespread opinion I reported in my book, *Life's Dominion*, that great art is sacred; he says art has great value, but only because it is or can be appreciated by human beings. He acknowledges that many people have a special reverence for an original painting as distinct from a reproduction – he was himself thrilled by a recent Vermeer show – and that this is not fully explained by the hypothesis that a reproduction cannot capture everything in a painting that contributes to its aesthetic impact. But he thinks that this reverence for 'relics' is a reaction for some reason hardwired into us (fortunately, he doesn't claim it had survival value in our ancestral savannahs) and that, as techniques of reproduction improve, that reaction might well subside.

He notes my suggestion that we delight in great art because we think it great, not the other way around, and asks whether we would have any reason not to destroy a Vermeer if we were satisfied that no one could possibly ever see it again. I think we would – we should not open the vault he describes simply to enjoy the explosion. Warburton thinks that whether it is wrong to destroy a great painting in these circumstances depends on whether 'the world in which the painting continues to exist unseen is a better one than the one in which it is destroyed'. But that is because he doesn't accept the category of the sacred or inviolable: the whole point of that category is to distinguish the rightness or wrongness of certain acts from any judgement about the goodness of the state of affairs those acts produce.[1] We can think it very wrong deliberately to destroy something of value without also thinking that the world would be a better place if it continues to exist wholly unknown, just as we can think it very wrong to destroy a painting even if we thought the world would not have gone much (or any) worse had the artist painted one less painting than he did.[2]

Warburton begins with an abstract philosophical assumption – that the value of art can lie only in its 'potential to be appreciated'. He then inspects his own more concrete opinions about and reactions to art and dismisses those he cannot square with that abstract assumption as 'vestiges of religious magic'. He might have worked in the other direction: he might have begun with his own convictions about the value of an original Vermeer, for example, and asked what abstract view of value and art he must accept if he is to retain those convictions. That different style of argument might have ended in the same place: he might have found reasons why he could not accept the abstract presupposition that art can have intrinsic value. But, at least in my view, those arguments would themselves have had to be aesthetic arguments, and their grip on him might not have been as strong as the more concrete reactions with which he started.[3]

## Richard Norman and the Sacredness of Nature

Richard Norman considers the popular – and royal – view that nature is sacred. He makes important distinctions: he notes, for example, that though many arguments for conservation appeal to the idea that nature is sacred, many of these cite instrumental risks of various intervention-ist policies, risks that can be identified with no appeal to the concept of the sacred. He argues that nature cannot be seen as sacred if that means that people must never interfere with natural phenomena to prevent catastrophe and to improve human life. It is impossible not to intervene, and immoral to intervene as little as possible.

But few if any people believe that nature as such is sacred. Many do hold the much less extravagant view I discussed in *Life's Dominion*: that parts of nature, like important animal species and giant trees, are sacred. Norman thinks even this an inappropriate claim because the sacredness of human life depends on agency, and though some non-human animals may have agency, species and trees do not. He does not say, however, why he thinks that only objects that have agency can be sacred: people who think that species are sacred do not make the mis-take of thinking that nature as a whole or species in particular have motives or purposes.

The question whether species are sacred may be only termino-logical for Norman, however, because he does think that some natural phenomena have intrinsic value, and he offers a very interesting account of what that value consists in. He thinks that nature's intrinsic value is aesthetic, and that it depends not just on the possibility that nature can be beautiful but that it can be sublime. He quotes to good effect powerful poetic descriptions of natural phenomena and suggests that these reveal the 'expressive' force that nature has for some people on some occasions. He is right that this is a common literary theme across the spectrum of quality: Macbeth's porter found a portent in a storm and Disney's Snow White found menace in the trees. But this relational value hardly exhausts the intrinsic value many people find in the natural world. For many years America's politicians have debated protecting the giant sequoia trees of the country's north-west. They disagree about how close to the sequoia forests logging must be permitted in order to reduce the risk of forest fires, for instance. But beneath the argument lies an important agreement. 'This is one of the few debates where everyone agrees with the objective,' the supervisor of the Sequoia National Forest said recently. 'These trees are a national treasure, the largest living and growing things on earth. They must be protected.'[4] The trees may be expressive to those who gaze up at them, at least in some moods and on some occasions. But that is not the reason they seem inviolable in Flatbush or, indeed, in Essex.

## Suzanne Uniacke

Suzanne Uniacke writes about the sacred value of human life. I agree with much of what she says: about the importance of distinguishing the question whether and why human life is sacred from the question whether it is ever permissible to kill a human being, for example. My argument about abortion and euthanasia in *Life's Dominion* turns on the difference. I also agree that I should have been more explicit in that book about distinctions and connections among the concepts of the sacred, intrinsic value, and inviolability. I do not believe, however, that I suggested, as she says I did, that everything that is sacred has intrinsic value or that everything that has intrinsic value is sacred. On the contrary I said that flags may be sacred though they have no intrinsic value and that knowledge has intrinsic value even though it is not sacred.[5] So I plead innocent to the 'equivocation' she charges me with. The connection between the sacred and the inviolable is no doubt more complex. However, I do think that to regard something as sacred implies *something* about how it should be treated: that it must not be destroyed except for the most urgent kind of reason, for example: perhaps only to protect something else that is sacred.

Uniacke concludes that I think that whether or not something is sacred is a subjective matter: that it is not sacred unless someone regards or treats it as sacred. That, however, is not my view.[6] She may have been misled because in *Life's Dominion* I mainly discuss the character of people's opinions about the sacred, and much of what I say is for that reason expressed subjectively.

She also questions my suggestion that the sacred character of human life lies in the intersection of natural and human investment: she finds it more plausible to think that it consists in what she calls life's 'near-miraculous' self-sustaining and adaptive properties. Yet every bit of matter – a particle of energy, for example – seems just as miraculous in its own way, while human life seems no more miraculous, even in the ways that impress her, than non-human animal or plant life, which few people think sacred. We might one day confront the question whether life – even human life – created entirely from non-organic chemicals would be sacred right from the start. It seems to me that, at the very least, non-organic life is not obviously and indisputably sacred, in a way that human life, made by God in his own image according to some and as the starry pinnacle of eons of evolution according to others, is.

## Notes

1  Frances Kamm emphasizes the distinction in her article 'Ronald Dworkin's Views on Abortion and Assisted Suicide,' in J. Burley (ed.), *Ronald Dworkin and his Critics*, Blackwell's (forthcoming). She thinks that my use of 'inviolable' is wrong because I accept that sometimes it is permissible to destroy what is inviolable.

2  See *Life's Dominion*, New York: Vintage, 1994, 74: 'I do not myself wish there were more paintings by Tintoretto than there are. But I would nevertheless be appalled by the deliberate destruction of even one of those he did paint.'

3  Or so I argue in 'Objectivity and Truth: You'd Better Believe It', *Philosophy and Public Affairs*, 25/2 1996, also available on various websites.

4  *The New York Times*, 11 June 2003, p. A16.

5  See *Life's Dominion*, 74, 73.

6  For my general opinions about the objectivity of matters of value, see 'Objectivity and Truth'.

# Index